T0316605

Cambridge Elements

Elements in Public and Nonprofit Administration
edited by
Andrew Whitford
University of Georgia
Robert Christensen
Brigham Young University

ORGANIZING AND INSTITUTIONALIZING LOCAL SUSTAINABILITY

A Design Approach

Aaron Deslatte
Indiana University Bloomington

Shaftesbury Road, Cambridge CB2 8EA, United Kingdom

One Liberty Plaza, 20th Floor, New York, NY 10006, USA

477 Williamstown Road, Port Melbourne, VIC 3207, Australia

314–321, 3rd Floor, Plot 3, Splendor Forum, Jasola District Centre,
New Delhi – 110025, India

103 Penang Road, #05–06/07, Visioncrest Commercial, Singapore 238467

Cambridge University Press is part of Cambridge University Press & Assessment,
a department of the University of Cambridge.

We share the University's mission to contribute to society through the pursuit of
education, learning and research at the highest international levels of excellence.

www.cambridge.org
Information on this title: www.cambridge.org/9781009101363

DOI: 10.1017/9781009105804

First published 2022

A catalogue record for this publication is available from the British Library.

ISBN 978-1-009-10136-3 Paperback
ISSN 2515-4303 (online)
ISSN 2515-429X (print)

Organizing and Institutionalizing Local Sustainability

A Design Approach

Elements in Public and Nonprofit Administration

DOI: 10.1017/9781009105804
First published online: November 2022

Aaron Deslatte
Indiana University Bloomington
Author for correspondence: Aaron Deslatte, adeslatt@iu.edu

Abstract: This Element explores the role of public managers as designers. Drawing from systems-thinking and strategic management, a process-tracing methodology is used to examine three design processes whereby public managers develop strategies for adapting to climate change, build the requisite capabilities, and evaluate outcomes. Across three cases, the findings highlight the role of managers as "design-oriented" integration agents and point to areas where additional inquiry is warranted. This title is also available as Open Access on Cambridge Core.

This Element also has a video abstract: www.cambridge.org/Public and Nonprofit Administration_ Deslatte_abstract

Keywords: local sustainability, strategic management, capacity, performance, local government management

ISBNs: 9781009101363 (PB), 9781009105804 (OC)
ISSNs: 2515-4303 (online), 2515-429X (print)

Contents

1 Introduction: Design Processes in Local Sustainability

Cities are cauldrons of complexity (Ladyman and Wiesner 2020). Any day in any urban space, people with diverse experiences and backgrounds will interact in ordered and disordered ways. They pass each other in the streets, synchronize themselves on the beltway, commit crimes and commerce, consume resources, and expel waste. People make thousands of minute and consequential predictions about their world. And their personal lives, health, and livelihoods are impacted by a host of socio-environmental system feedback, such as air and water pollution, the conditions of the built environment, and the quality of social or political institutions. As complex systems, cities are partially chaotic and partially designed – influenced by both nonlinear system changes and the institutional rules and norms developed to try and establish some order.

To help manage this complexity, local governments have traditionally organized themselves along a clustering of specializations (Leon-Moreta 2018). They employ police officers, planners, engineers, administrators, personnel managers, lawyers, and accountants. The institutions, rules, and shared beliefs that shape their behavior have also evolved to try and make human-environmental interactions and outcomes more predictable within these systems. Sustainability is often defined along the lines of balancing environmental, economic, and equity goals and outcomes (Portney 2013). This definition hopefully assumes policymakers and managers can forecast future system states, create plausible alternative scenarios, and effectuate strategies to reach or avoid them. However, it also overlooks the reality that humans are at best boundedly rational actors, and socio-environmental systems have a way of producing novel, unexpected threats.

Crises such as the COVID-19 pandemic have highlighted many governmental failures. In the United States, state and local governments found themselves without a coordinated strategy for combating the virus, with limited federal direction and tragically obvious inequities in how the impacts were felt (Curley and Federman 2020; Deslatte, Hatch, and Stokan 2020). However, local government pandemic responses also illustrated the importance of organizations adapting their capabilities. Local governments employed heuristic learning methods and adapted to rapidly changing conditions (Dzigbede, Gehl, and Willoughby 2020). They repurposed resources and realigned routines. They designed makeshift solutions to novel problems. If we define sustainability a bit differently, as collectively agreed-to measures of system performance, local governments demonstrated the ability to pursue a variety of tailored sustainability goals in the face of significant challenges. However, pandemics are only one of the myriad, sustainability-related threats we face today. There is precious little theoretical or empirical consensus about how public managers should systematically address these challenges.

This Element explores the role of public managers in design processes. Design processes are heuristic-based routines that foster organizational learning and decision-making. Drawing from systems- and strategic management approaches, this study focuses on two related research questions: *how are such heuristic-based design processes organized, and how are they institutionalized?*

The first research question should sound familiar to management and organizational theorists. The social scientist Herbert Simon defined designing as a process for devising "courses of action aimed at changing existing situations into preferred ones" (Simon 1988). Designing is what engineers do when they develop cheaper, electric generation and storage technologies that can be brought to market. It is what architects and urban planners do when they troubleshoot how to repurpose aging buildings and degrading "gray" infrastructure. It is also what local government managers do when they attempt to tackle complicated global challenges such as climate change. Designing calls upon the entrepreneurial abilities of managers (Deslatte and Swann 2020), entailing ideation, coordination, and creating public value (Barzelay and Thompson 2010). It is also high-risk, because it involves rerouting resources – material, information, and financial flows.

Local government managers have been shown to rearrange organizational routines, build capabilities, and problem-solve in innovative ways (Johnsen 2018; Rosenberg Hansen and Ferlie 2016). But as of yet, public administration research has not sufficiently developed a resource-based theory that can encapsulate the heuristic design processes of public managers (van Aken and Berends 2018; Barzelay 2019).

For instance, public administration scholars have long explored the connections between the strategic management of public organizations and their performance (Andrews, Beynon, and McDermott 2016; Bryson, Berry, and Yang 2010; Poister 2010; Stazyk, Moldavanova, and Frederickson 2016). Strategic management is often described as the process of identifying organizational strengths and weaknesses, recognizing threats and opportunities on the horizon, coordinating resources to develop and implement plans, and then adjusting as information and conditions change (Berry 2001; Bryson 2010; Bryson and George 2020; Bryson, Berry, and Yang 2010; George, Walker, and Monster 2019; Poister 2010). Because local governments must plan strategically to enhance sustainability outcomes, this literature holds important insights for managers. However, an acknowledged shortcoming is the disconnect between strategic planning processes and organizational performance (Poister 2010). Do planning processes matter?

To know this, we need to understand how managers use sustainability performance information to adapt to undesirable outcomes (Moynihan and Pandey 2010). Sustainability involves inherent unpredictability. Local government managers pursuing climate mitigation or adaptation strategies face the reality that the odds may not be in their favor. Political and managerial turnover can thwart progress. Moreover, their administrative and policy discretion – just like their carbon-emission footprints – can be driven by action at a grander scale. State and federal preemptions, transportation infrastructure investments, vehicle-manufacturing markets, international agreements, the halting transition of the energy sector to renewable sources, and a myriad of consumer choices all play roles in creating the system dynamics. Climate change, human migratory patterns, and material resource flows – all processes with stochastic qualities that are difficult to predict – interact in self-organizing, non-linear ways to impact local economies, development decisions, city budgets, and social outcomes. How do managers learn and adapt amid such complexity? They learn, like all humans, through heuristic processes, which we call designing.

The second research question should sound familiar to institutional analysts. To them, organizational processes resemble patterns of interaction among actors (Ostrom 2011). These interactions can be formally or informally institutionalized through the rules, norms, or shared strategies that structure organizational behavior. This is akin to private firms shifting their production boundaries. When a factory retools its production processes, it acquires or shifts resources to produce new outputs. Private firms retool capabilities when they sense looming opportunities or threats. When a public organization adjusts its own capabilities to enhance its sustainability, it is altering its inputs and/or outputs in an effort to gain some leverage over the complexity of its environment and improve some facet of its performance (Andrews, Beynon, and McDermott 2016; Deslatte and Stokan 2020). Thus, *organizational capabilities* are the managerial equivalent of production technologies (Zollo and Winter 2002). Organizations, and the capabilities they develop, are a product of the rules, norms, and conventions that evolve in an attempt to create certainty from chaos. Capabilities become institutionalized when they alter the expectations, incentives, and sanctions that guide organizational behavior (Ostrom 2011). Institutionalized capabilities can provide managers with durable resources, moral authority, and guidance to accomplish organizational goals (Zhang, Li, and Yang 2022).

Understanding this linkage between heuristic-based design processes and institutions is critical. For two decades, planning, policy, and public administration researchers have studied sustainability efforts in local governments. Cumulatively, these literatures have focused on the drivers of policy adoption

(Krause 2011; Mazmanian and Kraft 2009; Portney 2013), implementation and management challenges (Park and Krause 2020; Zeemering 2018), and the barriers to performance gains (Deslatte and Swann 2020; Opp, Mosier, and Osgood 2018). Despite this attention, important gaps remain in integrating these various policy commitments, activities, and outcomes. Surprisingly, there is little theoretical or empirical consensus about how public managers should institute processes for enhancing sustainability.

This study examines strategic planning, capability-building, and performance management as interdependent "design-oriented" processes for enhancing the sustainability of cities, and posits that they are collectively necessary and individually insufficient. This implies that progress can break down at many points for a variety of reasons. To elucidate these design processes, this study traces the role of managers as "design-oriented" integration agents to identify where additional theoretical and empirical inquiry is warranted.

The term "design-oriented" is taken from the 2019 book by Michael Barzelay, *Public Management as a Design-Oriented Professional Discipline*. Its central premise is that public management as a practice-oriented field should be refocused on design-projects and professional activities. Barzelay's book was itself inspired by theorizing on designing (van Aken and Berends 2018; March 2010; Simon 1996) and creating public value (Bryson 2018; Moore 1995). Defined as generative, critical thinking, designing is central to planning processes, confronting implementation problems, and adapting in the face of ambiguous or less-than-ideal performance outcomes.

As an issue lens, sustainability reflects perhaps the greatest combination of design problems facing governments today. To look at the future, crises are everywhere, and they are contagious: climate change hastens pandemics and exacerbates systemic inequity. The complexity of sustainability challenges facing communities, countries, and the biosphere is too great for the average citizen, planner, or scientist to fully appreciate; yet it falls to policymakers, public administrators, scientists, and citizens to find solutions (Ostrom 1983; Stokan and Deslatte 2020). To do so, public organizations must be adaptive, which requires trial-and-error learning, innovation, and a willingness to fail.

Institutional Contexts and Organizational Processes

Uniting organizations and institutions is not a novel ambition. Classic studies of urban service delivery initiated by Elinor and Vincent Ostrom (Ostrom and Ostrom 1965) produced sharp debates over public authorities and their planning capabilities (Howell-Moroney 2008; Lowery 1999). This skepticism focused largely on institutions, and the tendency of public administrators to favor bureaucratic centralization or consolidation over alternatives in which voluntary collective-action or inter-sectoral collaboration might be superior (McGinnis and Ostrom 2012; Ostrom and Allen 2008). This debate provides valuable guidance today for integrating current scholarship on management and institutions. Elinor Ostrom's approach defines institutions as the "human-constructed constraints or opportunities" that individuals encounter when they make decisions and reap the consequences of their choices (McGinnis 2011). Accounting for institutional contexts is critical to developing any causal understanding of the levers that managers possess to influence sustainability.

Ostrom and colleagues (1990) developed the Institutional Analysis and Development (IAD) framework to organize such a systems-based approach. The IAD, depicted in Figure 1, provides a conceptual map for organizing variables or features of interest involved in collective-action problems such as the sustainable management of common-pool resources (i.e. fisheries, forests, or croplands). The unit of analysis is the action situation in which actors strive to make collective allocation and appropriation choices, conditioned on their community attributes (e.g. socioeconomic conditions), biophysical conditions (natural environment), and the rules (legal restrictions, norms, and strategies) in use at the time (Ostrom 2011). The patterns of interaction within these action situations are nested within these conditions, evaluated based on some criteria (i.e. efficiency and equity), and fed back into subsequent action situations. Thus, the framework is dynamic and focuses on feedback. Management-led activities, such as planning, coordinating, and budgeting can be thought of as iterative patterns of interactions within action situations. A key point about the IAD and this working definition of institutions comes from the "rules in use" category, which reflects both formal (laws and regulations) and informal (norms, practices, and beliefs) rules producing regularized patterns of behavior.

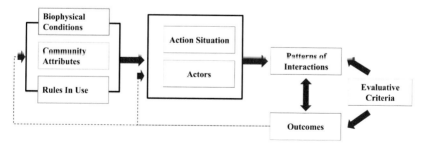

Figure 1 Depicts the IAD framework (Ostrom 1990), which organizes components of institutional systems for managing common-pool resources in sustainable ways. The framework focuses on the action situation in which actors may allocate resources and assess outcomes.

In democratic societies, much of what public managers can control in action situations is informal and process-oriented. Process innovations encapsulate the problem-solving that managers engage in as they develop strategies, implement them, and evaluate government actions. These process innovations may become legitimated as important informal institutional arrangements even within formal institutions, or "rules in form." While the IAD framework has been often used to study specific natural resource concerns (Deslatte et al. 2021), it also raises two important considerations for urban service delivery and sustainability.

First, public managers are nested within institutions at multiple scales, which constrains their available design choices. Managers operate within and have agency via formal political authority. Institutional designs shape organizational processes by conditioning the range of actions managers may, must, or must not take. For instance, Indiana differs from some neighboring states by limiting the home rule authority of local governments. Larger municipalities are legally prohibited from adopting council-manager forms of government, whereby stronger executive authority is vested within a city manager (Heyerdahl 1954; Rivas 1983). Similar to other US states, the Indiana legislature has also sought to preempt local governments from taking a range of sustainability-related actions (Bowman 2017). In a meta-analysis of local government innovation research, Walker (2014) has suggested that scholars must account for the joint effects of such external contexts and organizational capacities (Walker 2014). In an empirical test of Walker's argument, Zhang, Li, and Yang (2022) found evidence that statutory discretion – or the relative lack of preemption actions taken by the state legislature – was an important moderator of sustainability innovations (Zhang, Li, and Yang 2022).

Institutional constraints can be formalized at multiple interconnected levels, such as state requirements for the processes of local government budget adoption and amendments, but also via local directives (via ordinance) for specific policy actions of departments, and administratively designed assignment of responsibilities within and across departments for carrying them out. To explain policy choices, recent research has examined the role of institutional designs (Hawkins 2011; Krause and Hawkins 2021; Lubell, Feiock, and de la Cruz 2009; Stazyk, Moldavanova, and Frederickson 2016), regional governance (Yi et al. 2018), executive structure (Deslatte and Swann 2016), and differences between formal and informal collaborative mechanisms (Park, Krause, and Hawkins 2020). All these studies reinforce the role of institutional context on organization-level actions.

The second salient consideration is that design processes can also alter their institutional contexts. Design processes that facilitate learning and adaptation can alter behavioral norms, form new networks, and broaden the shared understanding of problems and solutions (Ostrom 2011). In other words, rules that facilitate design processes produce feedback on changes to community features and biophysical conditions. This, in turn, can facilitate changes to the rules. For instance, sustainability efforts often aim to improve economic conditions, natural resources, food systems, and public health or to reduce waste production, and inefficient transportation and land-use patterns. Organizations use design processes to ascertain how input variability (taxes, material flows, and information) and outputs (services, development, pollution, social welfare, and sprawl) lead to outcomes that may degrade or sustain these systems (Andrews and Boyne 2010; Piening 2013). When outcomes do not meet expectations, new institutional arrangements are often created to improve them. Design processes that alter the shared understanding of problems can iteratively alter informal norms and behavior (public awareness) and codify new policies, procedures, or regulatory regimes as formal institutional changes. While the IAD is generally used to control for these exogenous conditions in order to focus on the "fast feedbacks" or interactions of actors in specific choice contexts, the slow changes to exogenous conditions are critical to enhancing sustainability.

Few local sustainability studies have attempted to put these pieces together over timescales sufficient to study design processes and adaptation. Doing so is important for understanding how conditions or awareness of challenges or opportunities evolve (Anderies, Janssen, and Ostrom 2004; Leslie et al. 2015; McGinnis 2011). This study uses process-tracing to abductively identify three such design processes: *strategy assemblage, capability codification,* and *outcome identification.* It then investigates the extent of their institutionalization through heuristics or subroutines that facilitate learning.

Figure 2 nests these design processes within the IAD's exogenous components and focuses on how they may integrate over temporal and spatial distances. These design processes each produce intermediate outputs or outcomes (strategy content, outputs, and organizational attention), which may alter (or be altered by) exogenous conditions or context. This illustrates the interconnection (integration) of these processes referenced in public administration literature on strategic planning and management (Poister 2010).

Strategy assemblage (link 1) encompasses many of the tools of strategic planning and management, such as the assessment of strengths, weaknesses, opportunities, and threats (SWOT) and stakeholder engagement. Strategy provides a "means by which organizations can improve their performance and provide better services" (Boyne and Walker 2010, s185). Strategic planning and management are often conceptualized as processes rather than products (George, Walker, and Monster 2019), which produce formal, strategy-laden

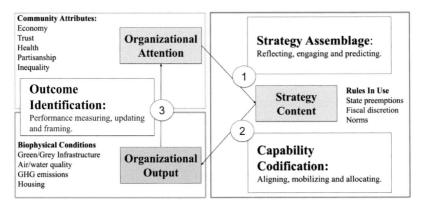

Figure 2 Displays how the organizational design processes of strategy assemblage, capability codification, and outcome identification are integrated across the IAD's exogenous categories. This conceptual framework can aid in the development of theoretical models and research designs to examine relationships between mechanisms and process-dependent outcomes.

plans. In the sustainability realm, these can be greenhouse-gas inventory reports, climate-action plans (CAPs), sustainability action plans (SAPs), resilience plans, and social vulnerability assessments. Cities may also nest sustainability goals within their comprehensive plans or economic development plans. An open question is whether these planning processes, formal articulation of goals, and implementation time frames successfully institutionalize the mission they seek to advance.

Capability codification (link 2) entails the sequencing of events and formalization of coordination mechanisms across administrative and sectoral silos to achieve goals. It involves the mobilization of actors and partners within the environment to marshal necessary skills, resources, and experience (Deslatte and Swann 2020; Krause, Hawkins, and Park 2019). These activities are ultimately aimed at securing larger allocations of resources to advance their unit-specific or organizational goals (Deslatte and Stokan 2020; Hawkins et al. 2016). Capability codification barriers include the sunk costs or path dependencies that policymakers, managers, and constituents rely on and defend (Deslatte and Stokan 2020).

Finally, *outcome identification* (link 3) involves collecting performance indicator or benchmark data, updating beliefs or predictions based on this information, and framing performance in ways to maintain or build organizational attention (Deslatte 2020a; Druckman, Fein, and Leeper 2012; Gross 2008). While performance is often considered within strategic management research, it is rarely given equal weight or modeled as a driver of subsequent actions (George, Walker, and Monster 2019). For instance, studies of performance information use in city sustainability have relied on cross-sectional surveys and cannot adequately explain why specific types of performance information are collected or how they are used in decision-making (Deslatte 2020b; Park and Krause 2020; Opp, Mosier, and Osgood 2018). Many of the sustainability performance indicators local governments rely upon are also factors beyond their control – or, extremely slow-moving social and environmental outcomes (Park and Krause 2020). Thus, outcome identification introduces cognitive biases and the rationalization that occurs as desired outputs and outcomes are subsumed by larger, context-dependent realities that managers may feel powerless to change.

Adapting systems frameworks like the IAD can help organize how researchers: (1) disentangle contextual conditions from mechanisms within individual processes; (2) build upon organizational theories that posit causal relationships between subsets of these factors or variables within or across these design processes; and (3) specify models with functional relationships between variables for testing hypotheses under well-defined conditions (McGinnis 2011).

Process-Tracing Methodological Approach

Process-tracing is a methodological approach in which an evidentiary record is examined to form within-case "causal generalizations about recurrent processes" (Mayntz 2004, 241). In doing so, the analysis treats design processes as concatenations of multiple activated mechanisms (Bardach 2004; Barzelay 2007; Beach and Kaas 2020). Rather than attempting to isolate and focus on individual mechanisms, the goal is to bin the range of potentially important management-led activities within the design processes. Observations about the evidentiary weight and cumulative effects of these processes can then guide future research.

Process-tracing provides a method for generating richer insights into specific cases where actions taken over temporal sequences produced observed outcomes (Beach and Pedersen 2019; Collier 2011; Fairfield and Charman 2017; Honig 2018). Unlike traditional statistical analysis, the approach relies on *ontological determinism*, meaning that outcomes occurred for a reason or reasons that are fixed in time and space. As illustrated in Figure 2, these three design processes each link to observed outcomes – attention focus, strategy content, and performance outputs. These within-case outcomes are deterministic, and the analysis focuses on the processes that produced them. Thus, internal validity is the goal, and external validity is the sacrifice (Beach and Kaas 2020).

The analysis follows a Bayesian-inspired two-stage evidence-evaluation framework developed by Beach and Pedersen (2019) in which propositions about a causal process are used to inform and assess the empirical fingerprints of the processes.

First, propositions about the three design processes were derived, drawing from the aforementioned strategic planning, implementation, and performance literature in public administration. Expectations for the actors, activities, and types of evidential material were identified, and beliefs were stated about the theoretical certainty of the process-supporting activity (do we have to observe the fingerprints?) and its uniqueness (if found, are there alternative explanations for finding it?).

Second, empirical material was collected to identify *mechanistic evidence* of the three design processes over a multi-year time scale (Beach and Pedersen 2019). An empirical record for three selected cases was assembled. The credibility of each piece of evidence was assessed, and confidence in the theoretical propositions was updated based on the strength of correspondence between evidence and expectations. Mechanistic evidence takes several forms: *pattern evidence*, which captures statistical patterns or predictions in the world (i.e. population growth forecasts of social vulnerability assessments); *sequence evidence*, which captures the temporal sequence of events thought to influence a causal process (timelines for implementation); *trace evidence*, which provides proof by its mere existence (a strategic plan); and *account evidence*, which delves into the contents or substance of empirical material (meeting minutes, oral histories, and interviews).

The raw empirical material was drawn from forty-two interviews with current and former employees and policymakers, public hearings, meeting transcripts and presentations, social vulnerability data, budgets, and a comprehensive review of planning documents, among other public records. Descriptive narratives and timelines of sustainability-related developments were created for each case spanning from 1990 through 2021. All evidence was evaluated to determine whether it confirmed or disconfirmed the primary contentions of each design process (Beach and Pedersen 2019). In doing so, specific heuristic learning activities (hereafter, "subroutines") within these design processes were inductively identified via two-cycle descriptive coding of interview and text data using an "organizational capability codebook" developed by researchers (MacQueen et al. 1998; Miles and Huberman 1994).

While process-tracing typically focuses on within-case inference, the Indiana cities of South Bend, Bloomington, and Indianapolis were selected as cases that could facilitate insights that can "travel across cases" (Beach and Pedersen 2019, p. 89). The cities share some similar characteristics – relatively low administrative autonomy (due to state home rule law), relatively high organizational capacities, and recent policy commitments to climate action. They each engaged in sustainability and climate-action planning, although the results to date have varied. Because process-tracing allows only within-case inference about causal mechanisms, Beach and Pedersen (2019) recommend identifying "deviant consistency" cases, where causes and contextual conditions are present but the outcome differs, to facilitate cross-case comparison. This study advances this case selection approach by treating the "outcome" of one process as the requisite condition of the next. Hence, the "causes" for our three interconnected design processes – attention allocation, strategy content development, and organizational outputs – trigger subsequent processes.

The state of Indiana is an ideal context due to its acute social and environmental challenges, institutional constraints, and location within a region of the United States that is under-studied by environmental researchers. The Midwest often gets romanticized as the "Heartland" and mocked as "Flyover Land." Indiana is politically conservative, nestled in a region that lags economically compared to faster-growing Southern and Western states without the burdens of post-industrial legacy cities (Hughes 2020). Many Midwestern states have experienced population declines in recent decades and suffer pernicious environmental impacts from their industrial and agricultural activities. Indiana releases more chemicals and pollutants per square mile into the air, water, and land than any other state.[1] In 2018, Indiana ranked second in the nation for coal consumed in electricity generation, and third in the nation for coal usage in the industrial sector. Indiana is the eighth-largest coal producer in the nation.[2]

Despite these challenges, dozens of Indiana cities have set a course in recent years to clean up their environments and reduce carbon footprints. Across the state, more than a dozen local governments were conducting inventories of the greenhouse gas (GHG) emissions of their communities and government activities in 2020, and more were planning to take the next step – adopting climate action plans (CAPs) that would map out strategies for achieving carbon reduction goals. Moreover, many communities were doing so via help from outside entities, most notably Indiana University's Environmental Resilience Institute (ERI), created in 2017 to provide technical assistance, planning tools, and some staffing capacity to municipalities attempting to address environmental and health risks.[3]

---

[1] www.epa.gov/toxics-release-inventory-tri-program.

[2] www.eia.gov/state/?sid=IN#:~:text=In%202020%2C%20Indiana%20ranked%20third,generation%2C%20after%20Texas%20and%20Missouri.

[3] https://eri.iu.edu/who-we-work-with/local-governments/resilience-cohort.html.

The following sections each key on distinct processes. Section 2 details the process of strategy assemblage that occurred in South Bend, spanning years of iterative efforts to plan new ways to address sustainability, resilience, and climate action. These efforts tend to be aspirational and often fail to change behavior until more formal institutional changes occur. Section 3 focuses on capability codification in Bloomington as a means for repurposing competencies (technical skills, experiences) and capacities (aggregate fiscal and non-monetary resources). Many organizational capabilities related to economic development, public works, and planning are fungible, meaning they can be reallocated to new uses (Levinthal and Wu 2010). Others present opportunity costs and risk (Bullock, Greer, and O'Toole 2019). Section 4 examines outcome identification in Indianapolis, where managers endeavored to make sense of social and environmental outcomes and frame them to advance sustainability aims. Section 5 concludes the Element by considering the extent to which these design processes are being integrated, offering future research directions.

2 Strategy Assemblage: Designing Conceptual Futures in South Bend

In January 2020, South Bend appeared poised for ambitious climate action. Former Democratic presidential candidate Pete Buttigieg was leaving the mayor's office, having championed the development of a "Carbon Neutral 2050" CAP, which called for a 26% reduction in carbon emissions by 2025. The forty-one-page strategic blueprint, Buttigieg wrote, "focuses on strategies that will provide the most substantial emissions cuts and will be feasible to implement in the near term." That implementation required shifting energy use and transportation patterns in the community, and was left to his mayoral successor, James Mueller, and a sustainability staff of one person.

By mid-March, SARS-CoV-2, the virus that causes coronavirus disease (COVID-19), had waylaid those plans. They were not alone. At least a half-dozen Indiana cities that had planned to produce CAPs in 2020 pushed back their schedules. By the end of 2020, South Bend appeared to be in full retreat, with the city shifting funding away from its sustainability office, the resignation of its sustainability director, and a failure to implement any major initiatives from its once-heralded climate plan. "We have a climate action plan that was adopted some time ago, and then we lost leadership with it. It's just been sitting there," said Krista Bailey, cochair of the city's Green Ribbon Commission, in summer 2021.

To most climate advocates, tangible progress on climate goals equates to top-line metrics such as reductions in either the overall or per-capita GHG emissions

(CO_2e) relative to a baseline year. But this entails a massive number of inter-related activities that feed into those measurables. South Bend's CAP commitment mirrored the original US Nationally Determined Contribution (NDC) under the 2015 Paris Agreement to reduce emissions by 26–28% (relative to 2005 levels) by 2025. In 2017, South Bend emitted 1.2 million metric tons of GHGs, with municipal operations accounting for only 3% of that total. Like most cities, its primary carbon-emissions sources were transportation and electricity use.[4] Any viable strategy for significant reductions would require transitioning off fossil fuels to support mobile and stationary emissions sources (vehicles and buildings), and increasing the energy efficiency of homes, businesses, and government buildings. In other words, any hope of reaching the 2025 target would require systematic infrastructure investments and behavioral changes – through energy and transportation decisions of individuals, firms, and governments.

However, South Bend's sustainability challenges predate its climate attention. The city draws its name from the bend in the St. Joseph River that presented an appealing landing spot for fur traders. The river powered the city's rise as a heavy industrial hub in the early twentieth century as companies like the Studebaker Corporation situated factories along its banks. Like many "legacy" industrial cities, South Bend began witnessing population decline in the 1960s due to the erosion of its manufacturing base and the slowdown of residential annexation. The river's pollution and recent refusal to remain within its banks present biophysical-system threats. Thus, the city's sustainability trajectory must be considered within the context of its social and environmental legacies.

Strategic planning and management research has demonstrated empirical evidence that planning produces positive outcomes in some contexts (George, Walker, and Monster 2019), but often overlooks the inherent unpredictability of complex systems and the inability of traditional "planning" to address it (Bovaird 2008). Strategies are only as useful as their power to steer governance and management decision-making. Cities have their feet in many public-service arenas, with varied departmental silos involved in their own specialized planning. Comprehensive plans are prepared by planning departments, illustrating current and future potential land uses in a community (Godschalk 2004). Capital improvement plans (CIPs) are prepared by public works or transportation departments to structure investment in physical infrastructure over a multi-year planning horizon. By contrast, strategic plans typically take a shorter planning horizon, aim to narrow the list of prioritized goals, and are produced

---

[4] http://docs.southbendin.gov/WebLink/0/edoc/279857/GHG%20Inventories.pdf.

by a variety of governmental units (Bryson, Berry, and Yang 2010). They can focus on an organization, a specific type of collaboration, or provide guidance to specific departments, ranging from economic development to parks and social services (Kwon, Berry, and Feiock 2009; Lee, McGuire, and Kim 2018). Finally, sustainability and climate goals may be incorporated into their own silo-spanning plans, which tend to vacillate between shorter and longer-term horizons, delve into broader societal or social goals, and provide fewer concrete directives for governmental actors (Alibašić 2018). Scholars have spent decades debating the merits of these plans – strategic, comprehensive, or otherwise (Bryson, Berry, and Yang 2010; Denhardt 1985; George, Walker, and Monster 2019; Poister 2010).

These ecologies of plans often do not speak to one another. They may or may not lead to development, refinement, and reformation of rules that incentivize or coerce behavioral changes. As a result, planning can often occur in a tokenistic fashion, disjointedly across land use, transportation, economic development, community development, and climate-action arenas. While planning may reflect the accumulation of shared knowledge, plans rarely produce changes to formal institutions and – at best – become guides for informal behavioral changes. This common deficiency highlights the importance for scholars and practitioners to distinguish planning as a product from its institutionalization as a process. While the former is ubiquitous, the latter is not (Hawkins et al., 2021). This leads to the following proposition:

Proposition 1: *Strategic planning is a necessary but not sufficient condition to institutionalize sustainability performance gains.*

In examining South Bend's efforts, the analysis inductively identified and assessed the importance of three heuristic-based subroutines of *strategy assemblage* – reflecting, engaging and predicting – each aimed at focusing organizational attention on the production of strategy content.

Depicted in Figure 3, strategy assemblage is derived from policy and public administration research seeking to link planning efforts to sustainability policy commitments (Kwon, Tang, and Kim 2018; Liao, Warner, and Homsy 2020; Zeemering 2018). Assemblage can be defined as "a collection or gathering of things or people," or "an object made of pieces fitted together." Thus, strategy development is conceptualized as a process of assembling people and resources and fitting together many preexisting parts, ideas, agendas, or policies. It is an effort to (re)design a conceptual future, to create new informal institutions, and it rarely starts from scratch.

The evidence comes from planning documents, hearings and public forums, budgets, citizen surveys, and participant interviews. These empirical materials

Strategy Assemblage

C Organizational Attention	Design process			O Strategy Content
	Reflecting: Environmental scan; assessment of organizational strengths, weaknesses, mandates; risk-evaluation.	**Engaging:** Elite/mass stakeholder participation, informing; employee, management consultation.	**Predicting:** Extrapolating; replication OR adaptation of object designs; consultation; data collection to convey conceptual futures.	

Figure 3 Depicts strategy assemblage as comprising reflection on mandates and the organizational environment, stakeholder engagement, and analysis of available cases or selectively identified data. These actions occur iteratively or intermittently as strategy is assembled.

are evaluated to determine whether they reflect pattern, trace, account, or sequence evidence of the design process (Beach and Pedersen 2019). Table 1 reports the actors, activities, and evidence types examined.

Reflecting

Reflecting occurs when organizations purposefully examine their existing or past planning efforts, with an eye toward organizational missions, mandates, strengths, and weaknesses (Bryson 2018). Fundamentally, it is a method for disentangling an organization's capabilities from its context. The actors involved are typically planners, managers, and/or select groups of stakeholders tasked with gaining a richer understanding of existing and future constraints and opportunities. Strategic planning scholar John Bryson (2010) details this process as a strategy change cycle, where self-reflection and analysis of strengths, weaknesses, opportunities, and threats (SWOT) can identify strategic priorities and help public organizations implement and evaluate them (Bryson 2016). Reflecting occurs via individual assessments, meetings, and forums where policymakers, managers, and stakeholders focus on the challenges and opportunities facing them. Reflecting can be used to accomplish other goals besides enhancing sustainability; however, it has also faced criticism as a formulaic exercise.

South Bend's empirical record demonstrates various periods of reflection. Growth and development have been central themes. The city's first comprehensive plan was created in 1961, focused largely on locations for government buildings, construction of thoroughfares, and recreational areas. Following the closure of the Studebaker Corporation in 1963 – a major regional employer – the city and county created an Area Plan Commission of St. Joseph County

Table 1 Heuristic subroutines of sustainability strategy assemblage

	Reflecting	Engaging	Predicting
Actors	Sustainability coordinator; consultants; dept. heads; internal stakeholders.	Sustainability coordinator; consultants; department heads; elected officials; external stakeholders.	Sustainability coordinator; consultants; planning staff; externs.
Activities	SWOT; informal meetings; public workshops.	Focus groups; online surveys; public presentations.	Data analysis of drivers and outcomes.
Empirical fingerprint	SWOT analysis in plans; meeting notes; interviews.	Surveys; summarization of feedback; interviews.	Data interpretation, forecasts in policy and planning docs.; case studies; interviews.
Evidence type	Sequence; trace; account	Pattern; trace; account	Pattern; trace; account
Theoretical certainty	High	High	High
Uniqueness	Low	Low	High

(APC) and engaged in several successive planning efforts focused on transportation issues. The formation of this regional body was intended to foster greater cooperation on growth and land-use issues between the city (which was losing population and wealth) and the increasingly affluent county, which was drawing many positive spillovers from the city.

By 1990, the city's population had fallen to 105,500, a 24% decline from 1960, while the county population had increased by 36%. South Bend had also become more racially and ethnically diverse and experienced a pronounced "brain drain" as more highly educated and highly paid households fled for suburbia. In response, the city embarked on an aggressive annexation effort to double the size of the city as a method for recapturing the tax base.[5] An annexation report noted that its declining population meant "a smaller number of City residents … must bear the costs of maintaining an increasingly higher level of services." The effort provoked political conflicts with potential annexes, resulting in the Indiana legislature effectively barring the city from involuntary annexations.[6] What followed was a decades-long struggle to reverse its economic and social decline by looking more inward at revitalization and community development.

The most significant of such efforts was a three-year planning process to develop a modern City Plan, which began in 2002 and was intended to map out areas for future growth. The City Plan adhered closely to established "smart growth" and "new urbanism" principles commonly espoused within university urban planning departments and by the American Planning Association at the time (Deslatte and Swann 2017). Its future land-use element emphasized smart-growth principles such as encouraging compactness, transit-oriented development with high walkability, mixed-use development and a variety of housing options. It also relied on new urbanist concepts for neighborhood-scale draws such as placing schools, shops, and parks near homes, lining streets with trees, and creating a sense of center for each neighborhood. The plan identified ten goals, such as encouraging "sustainable growth," a pedestrian-friendly balance of transportation options, "ethnic and racial harmony," diverse housing options, and enhancing the "quality of air, water, and land resources." An implementation chapter spelled out a five-year window of activities, although interviewees indicated this schedule was not utilized. The City Plan also never led to using additional financial or zoning incentives to encourage private developers to achieve desired land-use outcomes. As is common across the United States, it was never institutionalized. However, interview data suggest this planning effort did inform subsequent sustainability and climate action strategy development.

---

[5] https://southbendin.gov/department/community-investment/planning-community-resources/plans-studies/

[6] https://westsb.com/features/morepeople-five

South Bend formally began reflecting on its climate impact in 2008, when then-mayor Steve Luecke joined more than 1,000 other municipal chief executives in signing the US Conference of Mayors' Climate Protection Agreement.

In local public economies, land-use planning tends to evoke property-rights conflicts. However, the threat of climate change is a global externality that creates significant incentives for nations, regions, communities, and individuals to free ride on the efforts of others (Deslatte 2020e). Substantial efforts to reach "net neutrality" in emissions by 2050 in the United States or Europe can be overwhelmed by increasing emissions from industries in China or India. At a local scale, the costs and benefits of climate change cannot be internalized as they can via development or common-pool resource management. Moreover, the climate is a chaotic system, with "tipping points" or thresholds whereby large-scale changes in extreme weather with localized impacts become unavoidable (Ladyman and Wiesner 2020). Urban-scale climate action began in cities like Toronto and New York in the 1990s, but smaller communities have faced larger capacity-related challenges attempting to follow along (Hughes 2015).

Facing these realities, many cities have made "symbolic" pledges to address climate change, with some eventually abandoning the efforts (Krause, Yi, and Feiock 2016). South Bend's initial commitments remained largely symbolic for years. This provides an alternative explanation for why reflection might occur – to appease political constituents and generate reciprocal political or material support (Lubell, Feiock, and Ramirez 2005).

In 2009, Luecke formed the Green Ribbon Commission, a volunteer group of public- and private-sector citizens tasked with reviewing the city's administrative structure and recommending potential areas where it could make changes.[7]

Around this time, then-president, Barack Obama, and the Democrat-controlled Congress provided an impetus for many local governments through the 2009 American Recovery and Reinvestment Act (ARRA).[8] The ARRA included $3.2 billion for the US Department of Energy's Energy Efficiency and Conservation Block Grant (EECBG) program, which played an instrumental role in assisting many local governments kick-start their sustainability and climate-action efforts (Deslatte 2020b; Watson 2020). More than 2,000 local governments received funds, which could finance a wide variety of activities – from "greening" public buildings and vehicle fleets to building energy-efficient affordable housing (Deslatte 2020b). In South Bend, the Green Ribbon Commission recommended the city use its EECBG funds to create a Municipal Energy Office, placing responsibility for reducing citywide energy use in a single unit.

---

[7] https://southbendin.gov/department/community-investment/sustainability/
[8] www.usmayors.org/programs/mayors-climate-protection-center/

Concurrently, South Bend was grappling with significant community and biophysical system challenges. In 2011, South Bend entered into a consent decree with the US Environmental Protection Agency (EPA), which called for the city to devote more than $800 million through 2031 to reduce the two billion gallons of raw sewage its combined sewer-stormwater system dumped into the St. Joseph River annually. With roughly 27% of its population living below the poverty line, the commitment to cleaning up its sewer overflows left little financial flexibility to make infrastructure-related sustainability investments elsewhere.

> "Everything else was optional," said one interviewee.

Like other legacy cities, South Bend also faced significant degradation in its "gray" infrastructure, like roads and sewers. Its remaining population and tax base could not support maintaining its over-extended development footprint. Until 2019, the city's planning efforts were exclusively focused on land use, development, and economic challenges. The 2019 climate-planning efforts (detailed later in this section) drew from this record to identify what types of development incentives and regulations might be feasible.

Summarizing reflection, the evidence suggests city planners and managers considered existing organizational missions, mandates, strengths, and weaknesses as they initiated several successive strategy development processes. The evidentiary material, while substantial, is not sufficient by itself for making any claims that the planning process produced "strategy knowledge" that advanced sustainability goals (Bryson, Berry, and Yang 2010). As the strategic planning literature notes, organizations may begin down a path of developing strategies and never complete or formalize them. Reflection may be tokenistic and overlook or minimize past planning efforts. Cities may also produce plans without adequate support or involvement from stakeholders, which is the subroutine that is examined next.

Engaging

Engaging is the enlistment of stakeholders with knowledge of local contexts and personal stakes in negotiating successful outcomes. Engaging expands decision-making to new actors, through public forums, surveys, and other interactions with a broader swath of the community (Frederickson and O'Leary 2014; Portney 2005). Engagement is a way to both assess attitudes and beliefs, as well as to educate on sustainability issues. However, engagement is often exercised in a selective or perfunctory fashion after pivotal decisions have already been made internally.

South Bend made several intermittent attempts to engage citizens over the years. The city began a large-scale engagement effort in 2002 surrounding its City Plan preparation, which was intended to serve as a "guide for decision making over the next 20 years" and thus required "community support transcending any one administration or Common Council." Through a series of listening sessions, approximately 600 people were asked to provide feedback on what the city should look like by 2025.

> "Up to that point, [engagement] was not something the city had done extensively or done well," said one interviewee. "So that was kind of one of the guiding principles to the process."

The top issues citizens identified spanned several community challenges, including the need for diverse housing and commercial development downtown, the lack of walkability in the city's urban form, high crime rates, a declining property tax base, widespread vacant, unattractive land parcels and decaying buildings, and a lack of economic competitiveness. The report noted that solutions to its education and health/welfare challenges were programmatic issues that "the City governmental agencies may be able to promote or advocate for, but which the City cannot directly control." The only environmental topic to make the list of concerns was the pollution of the St. Joseph River, which had high levels of e.coli, polychlorinated biphenyls (PCBs), and mercury. Nevertheless, the effort is noteworthy for its exhaustiveness, with more than two dozen hearings and engagement exercises spread over parts of two years.

The overarching concerns over community attributes guided the efforts to prepare a sustainability strategy. By 2012, Pete Buttigieg had been elected mayor and prioritized blight reduction and community development in his campaign. The Green Ribbon Commission eventually was reconvened in 2014 to assist, and the Energy Office was expanded into an Office of Sustainability located within the Department of Public Works (DPW). While the previous Energy Office had been narrowly focused on implementing energy-efficiency projects in government operations, the Sustainability Office was given a broader scope to consider ways for improving natural resources such as water management, recycling, and waste.

Among its first orders of business was to gather greater input from the public on their own priorities relative to the economy, environment and social equity. Through an online and paper survey and community outreach events, the office collected 450 public responses to gauge baseline information as well as to "provide some basic education on and awareness of issues and definitions related to sustainability," according to internal documents.

> "We can do as much talking and listening as we want, but until people start really telling us what they're thinking, we won't really know for sure," Krista Bailey, who was then the city's sustainability coordinator, said during a 2014 radio interview.

The survey results indicated that citizens were concerned about the local economy, and city efforts to preserve natural resources and provide for a "safe, happy and healthy community for all." While citizens were pleased to see the office's formation, they also were ready to see results, Bailey said.

"They said 'Great. Glad you're here. Make a plan.'"

An internal "strategic sustainability plan" was prepared by the office a year later but never publicly released. It identified five goals, highlighted by the need to advance a more innovative economy, create safer streets and transit options and build neighborhood-level "identities" and community assets. A final goal of being a "net zero city" by 2050 came with recommendations for adopting LEED-like sustainability standards for city buildings and updating building codes for private developers to incentivize renewable energy and green building designs. It also called for eventually tracking energy use in larger commercial buildings, a so-called energy benchmarking and reporting program. Most of these initiatives would require formal action by the City Council to authorize and were not implemented. Instead, the staff went about attempting to build public support by focusing on energy savings and quality of life issues. This approach also frustrated a core group of community members who wanted to see more ambitious climate policy adoption and implementation, interviewees noted.

The Office was also expected to work toward the political objectives of its elected leadership. Mayor Buttigieg was interested in infrastructure, and successfully pushed through a $25 million "smart streets" initiative in 2015 to make South Bend's downtown more pedestrian-friendly and spur economic development.

One final difficulty with engagement was gaining the buy-in from other city departments, many of which had their own strategic or capital-investment plans that did not account for sustainability or climate-related activities. For instance, one of the 2015 sustainability plan's listed actions was increasing data collection to find opportunities for energy-efficiency gains in government buildings and vehicle fleets. South Bend lacked any government-wide policies for departments to consider sustainability goals in their own expenditures, such as vehicle purchases. There was no policy for building energy audits or upgrades, or asset management for replacing aging equipment. Making energy improvements systematically required conducting a facility condition assessment, whereby city-owned buildings are inspected floor-to-ceiling by a technical firm to assess anticipated future repair or refurbishment costs for mechanical, electrical, plumbing, structural, fire-protection, and other building components. The city needed new software systems for tracking fleet and facility energy use, and to convert the vehicle fleets to cleaner-burning compressed natural gas. However, it was a slow, frustrating process to convince policymakers and other department heads to take these steps. Informal institutional changes are often built on trust, negotiation, and reciprocity, and the office failed to get much traction.

> "People just really weren't listening to us all that much," said one interviewee, "or at least we didn't have the right ear or a big enough bullhorn."

The political messaging shifted after the city witnessed a 1,000-year flood in 2016 and another 500-year flood eighteen months later. The flooding damaged thousands of homes, washed out roads, submerged the wastewater treatment plant, and helped to increase the salience of local climate impacts. Elected leaders began staking out public positions supporting climate action. The South Bend Common Council passed the Cleaner Energy Resolution in 2016, expressing interest in reducing use of coal power and increasing investment in renewable options. As Mayor Buttigieg's political star was ascending, his presidential bid gave him a podium to sharpen the connection between extreme weather and anthropogenic climate change.

> "The biggest problem with climate change isn't that it's going to just hurt the planet," he said on *The Late Show with Stephen Colbert* in 2019. "I mean in some shape, way or form the planet is still going to be here, it's that we are hurting people. People who are alive right now and people who will be born in the future."[9]

Buttigieg would sign the state's "Repower Indiana" letter, calling for utilities to supply 100% clean energy. He also committed South Bend to the Global Covenant of Mayors for Climate and Energy. The Global Covenant, comprising over 9,000 cities across 132 countries, sought to collectively reduce 1.3 billion tons of annual CO_2 emissions by 2030. The city conducted a municipal operations GHG emissions inventory in 2016 and a community-wide inventory two years later. In April 2019, the South Bend Common Council passed a resolution calling for the development of a CAP. The city hired a Chicago-based consulting firm to do so, which included a more limited engagement effort (detailed in the next subsection).

In summary, South Bend made several efforts to engage internal and external stakeholders. The evidence suggests these efforts alone were not sufficient to motivate progress, given the alternative explanations for why managers might engage (i.e. passive information provision or "checking boxes" in strategic planning processes), the lack of buy-in from other city departments, and the lack of initial plan implementation. In particular, the empirical record suggests

---

[9] www.newsweek.com/pete-buttigieg-climate-change-religion-evangelical-1458137

the effort was less successful in engaging managers across governmental silos. This leads to the final subroutine of strategy assemblage process, which involves compiling the efforts of reflection and engagement through the analysis of future actions.

Predicting

Predicting involves a smaller subset of specialists attempting to understand how an organization's context and capabilities relate to observed and future outcomes. Ideally, reflection and engagement confer the evaluative criteria for assessing and predicting conceptual futures. This subroutine involves translating a community's history, context and desires into potential future pathways. Because time and resources are limited – and public administrators are risk averse – predicting inherently occurs in a boundedly rational fashion (March 2010).

Predicting involves interpreting organizational experiences and linking them to alternatives. Policy analysts or managers may learn from their own experiences and those of others (March 2010). Alternatives that have proven successful in another context are more likely to be repeated. And once an organization chooses an alternative, it is more likely to be chosen again. Because managers seek to minimize risks, they often mimic policy alternatives from a relatively small sample of "success stories" or "best practices." This type of extrapolation can prove challenging, because no two cases are identical (Bardach 2004). Extrapolation – even when analysts attempt to make "high intellect" or cognitive deductions – can lead to taking liberties with the causal nature of outcomes (Winter and Szulanski 2001, 2002).

In 2019, South Bend launched its climate-planning by hiring Delta Institute, a Chicago-based consulting firm that works with Midwestern legacy cities on sustainability planning. The firm describes its approach as taking the form of "an amoeba." Because cities have unique capacity needs, consultants attempt to fill in the gaps where they can, working within the resource constraints facing shrinking or economically challenged cities. As Delta CEO William Schleizer noted:

> We could be working with a small mid-size community that does community engagement really well, or with a larger community that's absolutely atrocious at it. It's surprising sometimes what you uncover . . . Is it community engagement? Is it the planning process? Is it the technical expertise? And at what levels? You might have a really good champion within a wastewater system that knows green and gray infrastructure really, really well. So, we don't need to provide that as much, because you have that capacity already there. So, we're like, "you guys have that covered, but let us think about how we then structure a planning process that works for you and we can utilize that."

The firm conducted a review of South Bend's previous planning efforts. For instance, both the city's land use and sustainability planning efforts had tried – and failed – to design green incentives into development decisions. Implementing the City Plan had depended on updating South Bend's zoning ordinance, subdivision regulations, and five-year CIP. However, most of the administrative and legal changes were never made. The city's zoning ordinance remained unchanged for more than a decade. The CIP was not updated to include smart-growth projects. The city's land-use strategies for "sustainable growth" had called for developing small-area plans for declining neighborhoods and corridors. This did ultimately happen for the East Bank Village, Howard Park, Lincoln Park, Southeast, and Westside neighborhoods. Three commercial corridor plans and a Riverfront parks and trails plan were also produced. These updated, small-area plans function legally as amendments to the City Plan and each reflect attempts to leverage prior planning efforts. However, a scheduled City Plan update was put off at the time.

> "There was a lack of political support for doing that," said one interviewee, who mentioned "planning fatigue," which had set in during subsequent years.

Beyond reviewing this past planning, developing the CAP involved validating the city's previous GHG inventories using the subscription-based ICLEI ClearPath software platform, and conducting a more limited stakeholder engagement effort. This was completed in June 2019 and consisted of interviews with ten stakeholders and four focus groups with members of the Green Ribbon Commission, business groups, organized labor, universities, nonprofits, and neighborhood representatives.

The evidence of predicting is both theoretically certain and unique – meaning the presence of the data analysis is sufficient trace evidence to conclude that strategy assemblage design process advanced sustainability progress. For the first time, the city committed itself to a timeline for GHG reduction. South Bend's climate strategies were also designed in ways intended to augment other land use and development planning.

To achieve a 26% net reduction in community-wide GHG emissions by 2025, Delta consultants noted their plan "leverages the most readily available policies and actions" and "takes advantage of the resources and capacity that South Bend already possesses, to implement immediate reduction opportunities."

For instance, the CAP called for an "incentive-oriented approach" such as using grants, loans, or credits to encourage sustainability projects, rather than regulatory action, given the slow post-industrial rebound of the city's economy. To support adoption of energy-efficiency improvements in homes, businesses, and industrial buildings, it recommended offering free energy audits, and adapting existing economic development tax-incentive tools – such as tax-increment financing and tax abatements used to recruit or retain businesses – to spur improvements to heating, cooling, ventilation, insulation, and lighting systems. It also reiterated the need for developing new building code ordinances with energy-efficiency requirements for new construction or major renovations.

Some of those ideas had originated in the internal sustainability plan but had been resisted for years.

> "Nobody wanted to require a developer ... to put forth more sustainable plans," said one interviewee. "Nobody made sustainability a criteria for giving out tax increment financing [TIF] or tax abatements. So, there were tools that we could have used that wouldn't have cost anything but would have required a lot of political will."

By the time South Bend was finalizing its CAP in 2019, it was also in the midst of a broader redevelopment-planning effort targeting blight with those property tax incentives.[10] Its Redevelopment Commission was finalizing four area development plans that would shape land use and public infrastructure investments for years to come.[11] This gradual strategy shift aimed at gaining new scale economies through repurposing under-used property to enhance the tax base and lower per-capita service costs. The plans outlined strategies for combating blight by encouraging "sustainable growth" through redevelopment in existing areas instead of the urban fringe, urban density, mixed-use development, rebuilding roads, providing more housing options, promoting "sustainable environmental management" of brownfield sites, and expanding the tree canopy.

These plans were developed independently of the CAP, although there were potential points of intersection involving public infrastructure. For instance, the redevelopment plans for the four quadrants of the city emphasized supporting a "walkable urban environment," the redevelopment of brownfield sites and reuse of existing buildings.

The CAP also relied heavily on external partners and community collective-action, promoting biking and walking through education and community partnerships, working with the South Bend Public Transportation Corporation to improve public transit options, and using existing development incentives to encourage denser, walkable development patterns. All told, a multitude of external partners would be necessary – property management firms, builders,

---

[10] www.southbendtribune.com/story/news/local/2018/06/02/south-bend-looks-for-growth-beyond-and-within-its-borders/46489933/

[11] https://southbendin.gov/wp-content/uploads/2018/07/River-East-Development-Plan.pdf

the chamber of commerce, and state agencies – along with repurposing existing planning and management capabilities to implement the CAP goals. The city would have to change its norms of "business as usual" for economic development.

> "Our goal at the end of these processes is for something to happen immediately and then over the long-term," said Delta CEO Schleizer. "So, we try to [take] the momentum from the planning process and make sure that it immediately gets transferred into an implementation process."

In summary, analysis occurred over a long horizon and was sufficient to support strategy assemblage. South Bend's CAP encapsulates some of the sustainability goals that developed throughout two decades of planning across multiple government units. City staff and/or external consultants engaged in varying levels of reflection on the organization and its strengths/weaknesses. They conducted in-depth analyses with available data. And they explored and imitated the strategies of other governments, through existing "best practices," success stories, and other governments experiences. The selection of Delta Institute as a consultant evidences the city's interest in tapping specialized expertise in working with legacy cities. Yet, the city's experience demonstrates how strategy content alone does not motivate regularized behavioral change.

The Results of Strategy Assemblage

South Bend has struggled since the pandemic to make headway on its sustainability goals. As of summer 2022, officials remained optimistic they would meet the city's 2025 GHG reduction targets. But South Bend continues to face significant community challenges in implementing its strategies moving forward. The slow progress can be attributed to a change in city leadership, the shifting of resources and attention due to the pandemic and social unrest (inequality), but also a longstanding reluctance on the part of managers across units to uproot or alter their existing, regularized norms, expectations, and interactions.

Implementation of the CAP was slated to begin in 2020. However, in the months following the COVID-19 lockdown, violent crime increased, and the local economy contracted.[12] Mayor Mueller and the Common Council opted to reprioritize short-term social needs to address the economic and public health fallout along with community unrest in the wake of national attention to the police killings of Black citizens. Multiple grant programs were refocused on

---

[12] www.kpcnews.com/news/state/article_a0eeedae-95c5-5abd-adfe-c5661fd85c86.html

helping existing businesses survive. The city developed a new "reasonable use of force" policy for police.[13]

Mueller also turned his administration's attention to infrastructure, passing a three-year, $25 million "Rebuilding Our Streets" plan focused on resurfacing and crack repair rather than redesigning streets to encourage more pedestrian use or biking.[14] The shift in focus extended to the operating budget. The mayor and Common Council adopted a $293 million budget for 2021, which cut funding for "strategic operations" and prioritized economic and social goals.[15] The budget cut funding for the Office of Sustainability by 10.5% – eliminating one part-time position and the consulting funds. As the budget was being finalized in late 2020, the sustainability director resigned. The Office was ultimately relocated from the DPW to the Department of Community Investment (DCI). While the CAP identified performance metrics and called for annual updates, the budget reduction, office relocation, and vacancy in the director's position effectively put those plans on hold.

In summer 2020, the city conducted a new community survey. It found the vast majority of respondents dissatisfied with its maintenance of city streets, sidewalks, and other infrastructure, its growth-planning approach, and enforcement of city codes and ordinances. A majority indicated they had seen no improvements in their neighborhood in the prior five years. The survey concluded the city was largely in the same place strategically as two decades earlier: with greater need for reliable infrastructure, economic recovery, neighborhood revitalization, and protection of vulnerable citizens.

Despite these setbacks, several interviewees expressed optimism. In his July 2021 "State of the City" address, the mayor touted the city's recent development accomplishments – landing a Trader Joe's grocery, among other new business starts – and pledged to continue supporting growth policies. He also noted the city planned to devote some funding from Congress's 2021 American Rescue Plan Act to affordable housing projects. Future plans also call for installing 3,000 solar panels on rooftops over two years and creating incentive programs for solar and energy-efficiency upgrades in homes.

> "South Bend is ready to take action. We must start taking bolder steps now," the mayor said.[16]

[13] https://southbendin.gov/wp-content/uploads/2020/08/Use-of-Force-Update-8.17.2020.pdf

[14] https://southbendin.gov/2021/04/22/rebuilding-our-streets-plan-implementation-begins/?fbclid=iwar3mk-v3pcdq7zhqft4fxcj9u-dxafywexeblrjio0_dspxy-h_rdm9nm_g

[15] City of South Bend, IN, Department of Administration and Finance, Budget Hearing #4: Strategic Operations September 2, 2020. (Accessed Nov. 6, 2020).

[16] www.southbendin.gov/2021/07/30/mayor-james-muellers-state-of-the-city-remarks/#:~:text=Good%20evening%20South%20Bend.,latest%20chapter%20in%20our%20story.

South Bend also filled its sustainability director position in late summer 2021. The new director set about reviewing past planning efforts, attempting to reengage with internal and external stakeholders, and implementing some of the CAP's initiatives. In January 2022, the city launched a community solar and energy-efficiency incentive program for nonprofits, which provided free energy audits to eighteen organizations and $400,000 to support solar installations and energy efficiency upgrades.

Additionally, the city was updating two small-business incentive programs that provide matching grants for façade improvements to encourage green infrastructure and energy-efficiency projects. Online training and certification costs were being provided for individuals seeking an entry-level solar photovoltaic (PV) credential as part of a larger workforce development initiative called Upskill SB. Finally, it was installing nine electric vehicle charging stations.

Because the CAP focused on incentivizing community actions, several interviewees said it made sense to house the office in its new Community Investment home. Policymakers "realized they really need somebody focused on the community, who knows the people, who knows the organizations, the neighborhood groups, everything else," said one interviewee.

Both of South Bend's CAP and City Plan documents were being updated, and climate action was expected to be a priority in the new comprehensive planning process. But, given the lost time, most of the initiatives from the 2019 CAP remained unimplemented.

South Bend's experience illustrates the design process of strategy assemblage, from heightened organizational attention to formal strategy guidance. Strategic planning scholarship suggests the process of strategy assemblage can positively influence sustainability gains, but only when it provides strong institutionally defined incentives along with tangible guidance rooted in historical context, community support, and viable alternatives for allocating resources. Strategies alone do not shift regularized patterns of behavior. The next section examines how cities may turn strategies into actions via organizational capabilities and their codification.

3 Recovery and Realignment: Organizational Capabilities and their Codification in Bloomington

In a scenic college town 200 miles to the south, Bloomington mayor John Hamilton christened 2020 with a clear-eyed sense of climate-action optimism.

The city had completed work on a $34 million park built on the remediated site of a former railroad switchyard. Its municipal water utility was implementing a $4 million green infrastructure program. Its bus fleet was going electric. Bloomington had equipped thirty-two municipal buildings with solar PV systems, with plans to extend the effort to the private sector. Across the progressive community of 89,000 people, tree canopy, trails, and pedestrian pathways were being expanded to transition the city's transit nodes away from its industrial past.

Like South Bend, Bloomington had faced a multi-year delay in translating its comprehensive planning efforts into development rules. But through several efforts to institutionalize sustainability and climate goals, that gradually changed. In 2018, when the city's Planning and Transportation Department adopted a new Unified Development Ordinance (UDO), it created density bonuses for developers to incorporate green building standards in new projects. The UDO identified sustainability, GHG reduction, public health, scenic beauty, and ecosystem services as core to its future development objectives. Bloomington had also taken a novel approach to administratively structuring its economic development and sustainability efforts, through a combined Department of Economic and Sustainable Development, which was one year into the implementation of a Sustainability Action Plan (SAP) that called for reducing community GHG emissions by 11% through 2023. The efforts had attracted outside acclaim. The Global Covenant of Mayors for Climate and Energy, an international consortium of 10,000 local governments, had named Bloomington one of 105 cities on its 'A' List for leadership and transparency on climate action. The city was given a Milestone Achievement Award for GHG Emissions Management by ICLEI, and the EPA had dubbed Bloomington a Green Power Partner.

The coming year promised more sizable commitments. Bloomington's first-ever climate vulnerability report was being developed to identify "climate related risks to people, infrastructure, and natural resources." And a separate CAP – which would be linked to a proposed 0.5% increase in Monroe County's local income tax rate – was in the works.

> "We have no Planet B," Mayor Hamilton declared in his February 2020 State of the City speech, which was devoted largely to climate action. "Does any one of us want to leave our next generations with a planet in tatters? With flooded coasts, extreme weather, disrupted agriculture and commerce, all creating global turmoil? We have to act."

Within a month, most of the longer-term policy and programmatic efforts were on hold. The pandemic forced the suspension of in-person governmental operations. Planning and implementation of sustainability initiatives would continue. Setbacks would occur. The pandemic exposed social and racial inequities, challenging a community that prided itself on its communitarian ideals. Following the economic shutdown and racial justice protests that gripped the nation, Bloomington tapped budgetary reserves to advance a "Recover Forward" budget plan funding both climate-action and social equity initiatives. However, the mayor's push for an increase in the local income tax to fund bigger-ticket sustainability projects would be voted down by the Common Council. By the end of 2021, council members were balking at the city's "underfunded" climate initiatives and pressing to administratively reorganize its sustainability staff.

Bloomington's experience illustrates the design process of *codifying organizational capabilities*. In Section 1, capabilities were described as the managerial means of organizational production. The strategic management literature can help unpack this concept as a function of resources and competencies. *Competencies* represent either core (possessed by many) or distinctive (unique) skills, expertise, know-how, or experiences that allow managers to strategically enhance organizational performance or value (Bryson, Ackermann, and Eden 2007). Cities possess competencies in a range of service areas, such as environmental and land-use planning, economic and community development, budgeting and finance, public works, transportation, and human resources, among others.

The aggregate level of resources committed to a specific competency is its *capacity*. As an example, a city's sustainability director may have developed skills in planning, GIS, or LEED certification, but only has the ability to function for seven to nine working hours, five (maybe six, but not advisable) days per week. This would constitute a capacity gap that influences organizational capabilities. But it is not a lack of a specific competency. Deslatte and Stokan (2020) note that when considering competency and capacity needs, public managers must determine whether economies of scale or scope are possible and whether the capability is essentially scale-free (which is rare). Thus, *capabilities* become a function of the two: the high-level strategic management potential, which encompasses both competencies and their linked capacities (Deslatte and Stokan 2020; Zollo and Winter 2002).

This distinction is important when organizations design solutions to problems and must decide, for instance, whether to hire outside consultants, new employees, or repurpose productive hours of current employees toward new tasks or training. They may decide to leverage core competencies to develop new services, or "compete on capabilities." As such, existing competencies may be adaptable to new uses. In this scenario, cities may achieve benefits via increasing the range of related goods or services they provide. In the private sector, firms can achieve economies of scope when they "leverage core competencies" such as their engineering, design, or manufacturing capabilities to enter new product markets (Besanko et al. 2009). Local governments may similarly enter new public-service industries as a function of their competencies and capacities. To distinguish themselves, cities seek to find synergies using existing capabilities that are fungible enough to reallocate to new programs or policy tools. Competencies that can be stretched for use on similar functions generate positive synergies and are more likely to lead to what Bryson, Ackermann, and Eden (2007) called *core, distinctive competencies*. In this sense, cities may pursue sustainable development as a means to distinguish themselves from the many alternative producers (cities) with similar core competencies (economic development tools).

From this, it follows that the codification of capabilities involves the process of creating permanent organizational practices or abilities for problem-solving. Codification of capabilities is the creation of new regularized patterns of activity via the combination of expertise and slack resources (Deslatte and Stokan 2020; Zhang, Li, and Yang 2022). In the legal and accounting fields, codification is defined as the arrangement of laws, rules, or procedures in accordance with a plan for achieving goals (Lauterpacht 1955; Llewellyn and Milne 2007). In cities, policies may be "codified" when the council adopts an ordinance or when electors ratify a municipal charter (Deslatte 2015). In economics and industrial engineering, codification has been conceptualized more broadly as a means of knowledge diffusion through economies, industries, or organizations (Cowan and Foray 1997). Knowledge codification requires translating tacit understanding or know-how into messages that can be more efficiently shared (Cowan, David, and Foray 2000). When knowledge is tacit within individuals or organizations, it is not as readily available or reproducible. Codified knowledge can reduce the costs of knowledge acquisition and retention through continuity as well as after management or leadership turnover (Simon 1997). Knowledge codification began receiving greater attention in the 1990s as it became clearer that the digital age was producing a "flux" of available information that both public and private organizations could utilize for advantage (Cowan, David, and Foray 2000; Zollo and Winter 2002). The need for greater attention to "big data" for organizational processes and decision-making has since increased by many orders of magnitude (Anastasopoulos and Whitford 2018; Gill 2021; Lavertu 2016).

In local governments, codification works not just through the adoption of ordinances but through the alignment of activities, mobilization of partnerships, and commitment of resources to specific aims, using acquired knowledge of practices or technologies. It is the routinization of collective-action within government and between public and private actors. Because codification of capabilities produces sunk costs, codified routines or processes can deter new legislators or adjacent department heads from adopting wholesale, inconsistent, or redundant policy changes. In other words, it can buffer against legislative meddling or short-termism in the policy process. Codification can be conceptualized as *a means to a means* – the passing along of the knowledge or ability to achieve organizational goals or objectives once their architects have exited the arena via political/administrative turnover (Constas 1958). This leads to the following proposition:

Proposition 2: *The codification of organizational capabilities is a necessary but not sufficient condition to institutionalize sustainability performance gains.*

In examining Bloomington's sustainability progress, the analysis inductively identified and assessed three heuristic-based subroutines involved in capability codification: *aligning, mobilizing,* and *allocating*. Depicted in Figure 4, this process involves identifying competencies and capacities and aligning them with strategies, sequencing efforts, mobilizing resources within the broader environment, and allocating said resources between alternative potential uses. Capability codification allows managers to create *complementarities* with existing public goods, services, or practices (Stokan and Deslatte 2020). Such complementary services or goods are beneficial because they are more likely to fall within the discretion of managers and are enhanced by the presence of existing core competencies. Codifying these capabilities is a means for achieving greater marginal returns on the initial fixed costs of acquiring strategy knowledge (Zander and Kogut 1995).

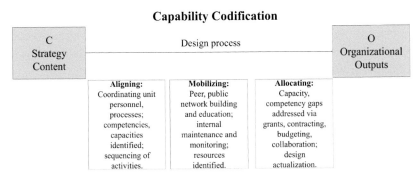

Figure 4 Depicts capability codification as comprising the alignment of personnel and processes across silos, the mobilization within peer, community, and funding networks, and the allocation of resources. These actions occur iteratively or intermittently as strategies are implemented and revised.

In the remainder of this section, Bloomington's capability codification is detailed through the challenges of implementing its Sustainability Action Plan (SAP) in 2020 and its Climate Action Plan in 2021. The evidence for this design process comes from planning documents, recordings of the Bloomington Common Council, committee and Sustainability Commission meetings held over Zoom during the pandemic, budget data, and participant interviews. Table 2 reports the actors, activities, and evidence types.

Aligning

Aligning entails the administrative organization and sequencing of events and responsibilities necessary to accomplish an organization's goals; the coordination within and across units; and the identification of competencies and capacities within the organization. Aligning is a necessary subroutine for capability codification, but it can also be explained by alternative motives, such as tokenistic or mandated coordination across units to placate elected officials (Krause, Feiock, and Hawkins 2016). Aligning alone reflects an incomplete picture of capability codification, and explains why quantitative evidence suggests that merely creating a sustainability unit within an organizational hierarchy may be insufficient to motivate progress (Krause and Hawkins 2021).

Aligning occurs when managers – typically led by dedicated sustainability staff – begin implementing plans by sequencing objectives or actions within temporal constraints (i.e. current versus future fiscal year), institutional contexts (i.e. programs or actions already underway; reporting requirements; timelines), and actor networks (lead department or unit). This sequencing of action and coordination across units facilitates the identification of available or needed organizational capabilities.

Many competencies local governments rely upon are core, such as economic development programs used for decades to recruit or retain employers via tax and regulatory policy tools (Rubin 1986). Adjusting these programs can create scope economies – but as the previous South Bend case demonstrates, they present significant opportunity costs that work against change. To pursue economic growth, cities may decide to continue to pour resources into their existing capabilities.

In Bloomington's case, the city had codified some capabilities prior to its sustainability and climate plan development. The Bloomington Common Council created an Environmental Quality and Conservation Commission in 1971, tasked via city ordinance to "protect human health and safety . . . prevent injury to plant and animal life and property" while also "promot[ing] the

Table 2 Heuristic subroutines of capability codification

	Aligning	Mobilizing	Allocating
Actors	Sustainability director; department heads; consultants; citizen commission.	Sustainability director; community partners; volunteers; mayor and city council.	Department heads; mayor and city council; community partners; sustainability director.
Activities	Coordination mechanisms (i.e. Team Green meetings); public meetings.	Working group/task force meetings; network formation; program/pilot rollout; public outreach.	Formative program/pilot evaluation; budget hearings, adjustments and approval.
Empirical fingerprint	Implementation schedules; assignment of responsibilities; resource requirements.	Public-private partnerships; program enrollment/outputs; online/media external communication.	Budget documents; evaluations; presentations on fiscal priorities; deliberation of allocational alternatives.
Evidence type	Sequence; account.	Account; pattern; trace.	Sequence; pattern; trace.
Theoretical certainty	High	High	High
Uniqueness	Low	High	High

economic and social development of Bloomington." This formalized institutional structure was authorized to advise the planning department on the impacts of development as well as producing scientific studies on pollution levels. The commission periodically produced a Bloomington Environmental Quality Indicators (BEQI) report that detailed current land-use, waste and recycling, air quality, water quality and quantity, soil conditions, and natural area/ecosystem indicators. Both reporting and subsequent use of BEQI information in planning processes require specific technical skills, drawing on the aggregate capacities behind those skills.

The city also created an advisory Commission on Sustainability in 2005, codifying a statutory definition of a sustainable community as one that "seeks to enhance the socio-environmental-economic well-being of the community while taking precautions not to compromise the quality of life of future generations." Its task was to propose new sustainability initiatives, advise the mayor, council, and city administration on sustainability-related policies or programs, and develop sustainability indicators that would be included in an annual "sustainability assessment" report. The city's sustainability director advised the commission, attended its meetings and produced information. The formation of a sustainability commission can bring new skills or experience into the organization, but also drains capacity – in the time and effort of city staff.

Many competencies are fungible and available for alternative uses; however, they are also non-scale-free (Deslatte and Stokan 2020). These limits to scale materialize via capacity constraints. For instance, Bloomington created a Green Building Program in 2009, which called for all newly constructed city buildings to meet, at a minimum, the US Green Building Council's LEED-NC Silver certification level. This requires either training staff to be LEED-certified or hiring outside consultants who could provide this guidance through building design and construction. The ordinance also stipulated that existing facilities would undergo a benefit-cost analysis to determine whether upgrading them to a LEED Silver rating would be cost-effective. Assuming personnel were formally training in benefit-cost analysis, this reflects a fungible competency with a capacity limit.

Bloomington further attempted to create economies of scale and scope when it created its hybrid Department of Economic and Sustainable Development (ESD). The department's physical space communicated "sustainability," located in a rehabilitated furniture factory, which also hosts a farmer's market, with a nearby Trades technology park, reclaimed rail-to-trail pedestrian pathway, mixed-use development, and an affordable housing complex. Its personnel focused on sustainability and climate action, along with economic development, small-business retention, as well as supporting community arts and cultural activities.

The ESD played a lead role in developing and implementing Bloomington's 2018 Sustainability Action Plan, which was organized around eight focus areas: climate change and adaptation; energy and the built environment; transportation; local food and agriculture; waste; water; ecosystem health; and city operations. Across these topics, the SAP identified 33 goals with 154 related actions to be taken, and assigned these actions to 21 different city departments, outside governmental authorities, or community partners – all to be completed by 2023.

Such a large-scale realignment of capabilities was initially sequenced to allow for each responsible party to take the lead in staying on schedule, although communication and coordination problems soon emerged (Carr and Hawkins 2013):

> "The process had been essentially having [a] person … try to think of organizations that would be well-suited to achieve given goals and then just kind of listing them accordingly," said one interviewee. "And then the struggle for the subsequent two years has been people arguing, 'I didn't know we were listed in that plan, that doesn't align with our current strategic vision.'"

Despite prior efforts to formalize environmental and sustainability-related processes, Bloomington's strategy development necessitated realigning structure, planning, operational processes, skills, and culture to forge new capabilities (Beer 2009; Poister 2010; Zeemering 2018). This presents some of the same challenges in shifting free-rider incentives of individual units.

Along these lines, the SAP called for the creation of a "Team Green" in 2019 made up of members from all city departments, which would hold monthly meetings to develop and implement an employee education plan related to each SAP element. Team Green would then produce an annual schedule of "activities, events and key messaging." Another two departments, Human Resources and Housing & Neighborhood Development (HAND), were also tasked with offering training to city employees on social equity, inclusion, and diversity. While the Team Green itself was organized, its membership shuffled as department representatives with different competencies came off and on, and its 2019 goal of implementing employee training on SAP goals never occurred. Nor did the citywide social equity training program.

Despite the setbacks, interviewees described the formalization of Team Green as a net positive for identifying challenges, improving lines of communications, and diffusing ideas.

> "I think sustainability can stumble when you have maybe one champion and they're trying to jam it through the rest of the organization," one team member said. "I think it's more successful if the organization starts to think about itself as everybody being a player in sustainability."

A 2019 SAP performance update noted many accomplishments and initiatives that had been completed or remained "in progress." A new GHG community emissions inventory and city operations inventory had been completed, identifying transportation, energy, and waste as the largest emissions sources. A "Solarize Bloomington" partnership with the Solar Indiana Renewable Energy Network (SIREN) had been launched to aid residential solar installations. A food-access survey was developed and a full-time local food coordinator with value-chain expertise was hired to help farmers and gardeners tap markets for their crops.

However, the "front loaded" sequencing of activities left many implementing actors without enough time to identify adequate competencies or capacities to complete tasks. For instance, while the Planning and Transportation Department had updated its UDO to strengthen its green building incentive program, the development of an educational program on sustainable development certifications and incentives – tasked jointly to the department and business community partners – had not occurred.

In all, the implementation report listed twenty-three actions sequenced originally for 2019, which had gone unmet. "We had a lot of things that were supposed to occur last year for no particular reason," said one interviewee in 2020. Because many actions were contingent on preceding actions, "if you're not able to do one thing, then the entire set of actions falls apart."

The experience with SAP implementation led Bloomington managers to revise their approach as they developed the CAP throughout 2020 and into 2021. The CAP identified a goal of reducing GHG emissions 25% from 2018 levels by 2030 (or 40% from 2005 levels) and achieve carbon neutrality by 2050. To accomplish this, the plan identified changes that would have to be adopted in transportation, energy use in buildings and homes, waste management, and water systems, among others. When the plan was publicly unveiled in late 2020, a draft implementation chapter had identified agencies, departments, and community partners with either primary or supporting responsibility for taking 266 different actions thatwould have to occur within eight years. However, the city and its consultants ultimately scrapped the implementation chapter after partners balked. Negotiating firm deadlines and responsibilities for each action proved to be too onerous given the uncertainty surrounding the pandemic and differing capacities across departments, according to interviews.

> "It wasn't going to be passed if we went the route that it was going," said one interviewee.

With the implementation chapter gone, the CAP was approved by the Bloomington Common Council on April 22, 2021 – Earth Day. However, with more ambiguous responsibilities assigned to actions, Bloomington managers were left to find new incentives to motivate implementing parties and negotiate actions with individual groups or city departments.

> "It just allows more flexibility. If [a] department is going a different direction because of any reason, they're not obligated to supposedly achieve something in a timeframe that no longer makes sense," said one interviewee. "That gives us more flexibility in saying that [if] partners can change over time, timelines should change. We can reorient the sequencing."

In summary, there is circumstantial evidence that aligning supported the codification of new capabilities. Aligning involves identifying existing or needed competencies and capacities, and sequencing actions that need to occur to implement strategy goals. It is about identifying core and distinctive competencies along with those that are lacking but necessary to accomplish goals. For public managers, this is a time-consuming and flustering prerequisite that leads to the need to determine where and how to mobilize external partners to help fill in the gaps.

Mobilizing

Mobilizing involves two main activities: identifying partners within an organization's environment; and motivating or leveraging their participation in collaborative efforts. It may be initiated or led by public managers, but it requires the involvement of a broader range of external actors. Because many of the goals of local sustainability span organizational boundaries, collaboration has been widely espoused as a method of overcoming spillover-related sustainability problems (Krause, Hawkins, and Park 2019; Swann 2017). For sustainability directors, this may be membership in the Urban Sustainability Directors Network (Anderson et al. 2015). Organizations such as the ICLEI Climate Protection program, USGBC and the US Conference of Mayors' Climate Mayors network formed to diffuse insights, technical know-how, and practical sustainability-related experiences (Yi, Krause, and Feiock 2017). Regional "green" networks such as the Greenest Region Compact (GRC) in metropolitan Chicago or Green Umbrella in Cincinnati are also examples of voluntary policy networks where local governments collectively attempt to overcome risks associated with climate action and sustainability (Stokan and Deslatte 2020).

But not every local government exists in a major metropolitan region with many potential collaborative partners (Levesque, Bell, and Calhoun 2017). Mobilizing also involves reliance on civic community partners, nonprofits, and business organizations for help spearheading changes. In the collaboration literature, embedding commitments across public and private organizations creates opportunities for facilitating employee routines for dialogue, information exchange and "principled engagement" (Bingham, Nabatchi, and O'Leary 2005; Emerson, Nabatchi, and Balogh 2012; Park, Krause, and Hawkins 2020). At a minimum, this requires iterative interactions leading to shared expectations, trust, and agreement on sustainability goals, timelines, barriers, and plausible or innovative ideas for dealing with them.

A central component of Bloomington's CAP focused on achieving greater energy efficiency in residential, commercial, and industrial buildings, as well as generating more of the energy they consume from renewable sources. According to the city's 2018 inventory, the built environment – both through on-site fossil-fuel burning for heating and cooking and off-site burning for energy production – accounted for 77% of the city's carbon emissions (38% from residential consumption, 44% from commercial and government buildings, and 18% from industrial uses). Meanwhile, its primary electric utility, Duke Energy, derived 61% of its electric generation from coal. While Duke had adopted energy-portfolio plans for a gradual drawdown of that fuel type through 2037, that target was not aggressive enough to meet Bloomington's GHG reduction goal. Thus, the city's strategy also called for increasing distributed (on-site) renewable energy production citywide and improving energy-efficiency measures in buildings.

This presented a sizable mobilization challenge. By 2021, Bloomington had maxed out the roof space on government-owned buildings available for solar panels. Through a Solarize Bloomington initiative launched in 2016, the city had put thirty-four solar installations on government facilities, which offset roughly 70% of its electric use (excluding its water utility). Pivoting from a municipal solar focus to incentivizing wider residential and commercial solar required outreach to property owners, partnerships with financial institutions, and education/training of contractors to conduct the work.

> "The city can only do so much," said Bloomington ESD Director Alex Crowley. "The private sector has to have a big role, and if they're not on board, you're going to be able to chip away, but not very aggressively."

The inspiration for Bloomington's solar efforts began at the grassroots. Solarize Bloomington started in 2016 with high school students going door-to-door to gauge interest in photovoltaic systems installation. From there, the initiative morphed into an effort to educate residents on the costs and benefits of solar through information sessions held by Solar Indiana Renewable Energy Network (SIREN), a project of a Bloomington nonprofit called the Center for Sustainable Living. A year later, the city had committed $13 million to placing solar panels on its own buildings, and the Center had launched an Indiana Solar for All effort to find solar grants for lower-income households.

Meanwhile, the mayor had convened a working group of community development organizations to study how the city could attract capital from outside Community Development Financial Institutions (CDFI), private lenders that focus efforts on blighted or poorer communities. Typically, CDFIs are hesitant to move into smaller markets because of the difficulties in scaling up capital investments there without a broad base of technical support and gap financing for potential borrowers. The working group concluded it was not feasible to start a CDFI in Bloomington or entice an existing CDFI to open shop there. So, at the city's urging, several local groups opted to create a nonprofit called CDFI Friendly Bloomington. This entity would do the legwork of finding contractors, making connections and investing its own capital in order to entice outside CDFIs to make loans in Bloomington.

The mobilization of different actors built on the lessons Bloomington had learned from its solar efforts, which had centered on connecting residents to qualified contractors. Up-front solar costs also presented social equity barriers and required managers to identify and enlist multiple potential lenders interested in filling gaps in the marketplace for solar. Homeowners would typically have to self-finance solar installations or seek out financing options through existing lender relationships using the financial equity in their homes. For many households, an investment of up to $15,000 for solar was out of reach.

As part of its "Recover Forward" 2021 budget, Bloomington set aside $100,000 to pilot a new Bloomington Green Home Improvement Program (BGHIP) to finance energy-efficiency upgrades in owner-occupied single-family homes. The city's experience from its Solarize outreach suggested homeowners lost interest if obvious financing options were not available. Once solar projects were completed, there were no additional avenues to steer them toward other energy-efficiency improvements. The BGHIP created a pilot, reduced-interest loan fund that could be used to cover a wider array of eligible energy upgrades, including HVAC repairs, water heating, lighting, appliances, and even electric vehicle charging stations. Households with annual incomes below $100,000 would also be eligible for a $1,000 rebate once a project was completed. The project was a collaboration with CDFI Friendly Bloomington, and loans were provided through the Colorado-based Clean Energy Credit Union. This allowed the city to stay out of the loan management business, where it lacked both capacity and competencies.

To plug another gap in the market, the city budgeted $100,000 for a Solar & Energy Efficiency Loan (SEEL) pilot program to help finance energy-efficiency projects at nonprofits and community institutions such as schools, libraries, and medical facilities. Again, the city relied on CDFI Friendly Bloomington to entice a larger Chicago-based CDFI (IFF) to enter the market and finance loans. Because the city had difficulties finding contractors willing to do the energy assessments in smaller buildings, IFF opted to provide that service during the program's start-up.

Launching these programs was made possible through the overlapping alignment and mobilization of partnerships, according to interviewees. Identifying the technical competencies needed was not enough – finding incentives that can overcome collective-action challenges was necessary.

> "There weren't a ton of examples," said one interviewee. "I mean, we just basically said, 'here's what we're trying to go for' and worked backwards. And, so it's been a little bit bumpy trying to anticipate what the problems will be."

In summary, mobilizing entails identifying and motivating partners who possess competencies or capacities the organization needs to fulfill its mission. Policymakers and managers mobilized actors external to the organization to fill their capacity and competency needs. While some financial capacity was a prerequisite to launch the solar pilot programs, Bloomington initially lacked internal expertise on solar technologies and the staff capacity and competencies to handle the management or servicing of loans. While the programs were launched as pilots as a means of reducing risk, their survival also hinged on identification of stable financial and material resource commitments. This is a heuristic subroutine called allocating.

Allocating

Aligning and mobilizing both facilitate *allocating* fiscal and human resources toward new pursuits. Allocation is often the most visible and difficult part of codifying organizational capabilities. Financial resources in local governments produce dedicated constituencies and path dependencies. There is a rich public choice literature exploring competition between pressure groups for favorable treatment in local government policy and funding (Becker 1983; Lubell, Feiock, and Ramirez 2005; Ostrom and Ostrom 2019; Pennington 2000; Teske et al. 1993). This political market literature treats government actors as suppliers of public policies and has tended to find historically that stable equilibria emerge favoring wealthier or more privileged interests over more diffuse groups (Feiock, Tavares, and Lubell 2008).

Recent evidence suggests that local government managers play a moderating role in the resource commitments of cities (Deslatte 2018; Deslatte, Swann, and

Feiock 2017; Deslatte, Tavares, and Feiock 2016). However, this work has largely relied upon proxy measures of how managerial authority is institutionally structured within local governments (Carr 2015; Deslatte 2018), and has rarely examined the actual processes, methods, or approaches managers use to steer resource allocation. One exception is Hawkins and colleagues' (2016) article, which found that US cities were more likely to commit staff and fiscal resources to sustainability when they had prioritized social equity goals and received technical support from green groups such as ICLEI (Hawkins et al. 2016).

Conversely, prioritization of economic goals such as business recruitment can produce dedicated constituencies and a hesitancy on the part of policymakers to reallocate resources to sustainability (Deslatte and Stokan 2020). As previously noted, organizational capabilities can be fungible but are also non-scale-free. This means the dedication of time, energy, or effort to one set of tasks limits their use elsewhere (Levinthal and Wu 2010). Yet, without reallocating resources to new sustainability missions, large-scale gains are often not possible (Deslatte and Stokan 2017).

Prior to the pandemic, more than a dozen Indiana communities had planned to allocate resources to developing and implementing climate policies in 2020. Instead, many had to adapt on the fly, continuing to make gains in some areas while experiencing delays, setbacks, and frustrations in others. In the process, the health, social, and economic needs of community groups became the principal priority. Cities were faced with tragic yet predictable social consequences of intergenerational disinvestment and discrimination against minority groups. The pandemic presented a stress test especially salient for sustainability managers – often, the harbingers of the overlapping health and economic consequences of climate change.

In August 2020, the Bloomington Common Council agreed to appropriate $2 million of its budget reserves to the first phase of the "Recover Forward" plan, which supported economic programs like job incentives for small businesses, energy-efficiency upgrades for commercial and residential projects, and a range of social support efforts – from down payment assistance for affordable housing homeowners to expanding broadband Internet access in poorer neighborhoods. The city's 2021 budget devoted $4 million more from reserves to advance "racial, economic, and climate justice" projects, such as the solar/energy efficiency loan programs.

But the plan's proponents also suffered a significant setback in September 2020, when the council narrowly voted down a plan to raise the Local Income Tax (LIT) by 0.25%, which would have created a dedicated funding stream ($4 million annually) for climate, economic, and social justice initiatives.

"We certainly face enormous challenges now and for the foreseeable future – COVID, climate change, racial justice, growing economic disruptions and inequality," Mayor Hamilton told the council. "If we want to seriously recover forward, we have to have resources to do so."

Despite the vote, the city was able to press forward with its Phase 3 Recover Forward plan in 2022, using $1.4 million from the American Rescue Plan Act (ARPA) for enhancing funding for its small-business support, as well as assistance for local food growers and artists. A majority of that total ($750,000) was targeted toward expanding its solar and energy-efficiency loan programs.

It is important to note that allocating is not just a result of funding windfalls or economic growth; as a management-supported function, it hinges on making a successful case for shifting resources and tends to happen iteratively as administrators incrementally assess and strategically align priorities for policymakers. Without significant effort to schedule the implementation steps and line up partners and technical know-how, allocating fiscal resources for the continuation or expansion of sustainability activities would be extremely difficult, interviewees said. As an example, the Bloomington City Council ultimately voted again in 2022 to pass a local income tax increase, $1.6 million of which would be devoted to climate action.

The challenges facing Bloomington and every community attempting to make dramatic changes to its sustainability outcomes remain the "sunk costs" of prior investments and the indeterminant scale and scope economies of action. It is possible the capabilities Bloomington has developed and realigned will be enhanced as successful rollouts of programs generate greater tolerance for risks and support for larger investments across government units and within the community. However, many of the 266 action items included in the city's CAP come with indeterminate price tags, lack specific outcome measures that can be assessed, and thus have no explicit connections to any current capabilities. It is also possible the city will be unable to develop sufficient scale economies to expand community-based solar programs.

"Some of these programs are brand new this year, so we're testing them out right now," ESD Director Crowley explained to the Council during August 2021 budget hearings. "We will only double-down and reinvest in programs which are proving successful."

This cautiousness on the part of managers presented downside risk, particularly by frustrating several council members during Bloomington's 2022 budget deliberations. By initiating only a handful of those 266 action items, several councilors argued, the city was unlikely to meet its 2030 climate goals. Two City Council members also pressed for shaking up the department and moving the lead sustainability position out of the ESD and placing it directly under the mayor. Such formal institutional changes are common across local governments (Krause and Hawkins 2021), reflecting the difficulty in adapting existing institutional arrangements to confront new challenges.

> "I just really don't think we have capacity to implement the plan we've adopted," Councilor Matt Flaherty said in an interview.

In summary, allocating resources depends on management-led alignment and mobilization of partners and activities to overcome the risk-aversion endemic to public organizations. There is evidence that policymakers made resource allocations in tandem with the guidance and argumentation of managers. Allocating is vital to codifying capabilities. However, allocating is often misconstrued as the beginning of an implementation effort when, in fact, it is a cyclical, ongoing part of the capability codification process, supported by both aligning and mobilizing. Allocating is more likely to occur when managers have sequenced activities and started small, justifying the worthiness of larger investments. Allocating public resources is also more likely when leveraged with external resources and partnerships. While financial barriers are often cited as a reason for why sustainability progress is lacking, Bloomington's case illustrates how aligning and mobilizing can aid in overcoming the allocation barrier.

The Results of Capability Codification

Bloomington entered 2022 better positioned to advance its sustainability objectives, despite the lingering pandemic fallout. The evidence supports the central proposition that codifying organizational capabilities is both necessary and sufficient for translating sustainability strategies into organizational outcomes. Although setbacks occurred, the alignment of personnel and activities, the mobilization of network partners, and the search and reallocation of resources all occurred – evidence of newly codified, if informal, capabilities. But the uncertainty surrounding the city's future conditions and commitment to climate action was also on display in its budget deliberations, highlighting both demands for formalized institutional changes and the reduced margin for error local governments face in order to achieve climate goals.

The city adopted its CAP and expanded its community solar program in the midst of the pandemic. In its 2022 budget negotiations, Bloomington council members successfully pushed the mayor's office to increase funding for CAP implementation to $1.25 million. The Council ultimately voted again in 2022 to pass the local income tax, part of which would create a recurring funding source for climate action. However, the city's revenue streams from activities like parking and business taxes have declined. Future fiscal uncertainty motivated sustainability staff to take a cautious approach to creating new initiatives, while frustrating some policymakers who want more aggressive implementation. As one city council member noted about the CAP's long list of objectives, "We need dollar signs next to these items."

In some ways, the successful development of strategies and efforts to marshal resources in 2021 only drew a clearer distinction between the "low-hanging fruit" sustainability actions cities tend to pursue and the investments required to substantially curb GHG emissions in coming years. Bloomington had long since completed many of the initial actions cities take to kick-start sustainability progress and produce quick results. What remains are the harder choices for incentivizing developers and households to make larger adjustments. That includes larger transportation and infrastructure investments, changes to its built environment, as well as greater coordination across government silos. As Councilor Flaherty noted in an interview:

> A lot of [what is happening now] is program implementation, and it doesn't necessarily require a lot of dollars. Though, inevitably there will be some things we need to be doing in the transportation contexts that are capital intensive and probably some other areas too. So, there's capacity, there's funding. And then finally, there's this sort of political question of like, are the right folks communicating? Is this cross-cutting throughout the city's organization? I have concerns about that, too.

Bloomington's case also highlights the collaboration risks inherent in sustainability efforts, such as coordination and monitoring costs that are incurred not just across government units, but throughout a community. These risks tend to weigh heavily on loss-averse public managers and help explain their go-slow tendencies in initiating new programs (Deslatte, Swann, and Feiock 2020). For instance, Bloomington's staff acknowledged that across both the 154 SAP action items and 266 actions in the CAP, many activities could fall by the wayside as budgets, networks, and agency demands change in coming years.

> "This takes internal partnerships. It takes external partnerships," Crowley told councilors in summer 2021. "We need to be flexible. ... Hopefully, we are able to implement these things. But in some cases, we need to be prepared that we won't."

Climate change and the myriad consequences for society create uncertainty. Ultimately, public managers confronting these challenges must bring some predictive accuracy into policy and public forums to motivate ongoing action. This emphasizes the importance of generating accurate and actionable performance information that helps managers collect, interpret, and frame performance outcomes, maintain momentum, and help policymakers adjust to changing conditions.

4 Reverse-Engineering Performance: Outcome Identification in Indianapolis

Perhaps no place saw pre-pandemic hopes dashed like Indianapolis.

Before COVID-19, Indiana's capital city had been one of 25 communities selected in 2018 for the Bloomberg Philanthropies' American Cities Climate Challenge (ACCC), splitting $70 million in technical assistance and other resources. The two-year challenge concentrated generally on two policy areas cities have some control over – the energy use of buildings and transportation. In Indianapolis, the challenge was further focused on three legislative initiatives (building energy benchmarking and transparency; transit-oriented development; and electric-vehicle readiness) along with five "programmatic" areas (such as piloting a resilience hub and making transit more equitable). The challenge effectively required codifying capabilities and provided significant fiscal capacity and technical competencies – such as expert consultants and network connections with sustainability staff in other ACCC cities like Orlando, Chicago, and St. Louis.

Alongside its participation in the challenge, Indianapolis staff had completed the city's first "Thrive Indianapolis" (hereafter, Thrive) resilience and sustainability action plan in 2019. Its development included an innovative, seven-month public engagement effort in which consultants and city staff adopted a community-organizing model for reaching vulnerable neighborhoods, fanning out to get feedback at block parties, community centers, and neighborhood meetings. They conducted focus groups with the homeless, citizens reentering the community from prison, and low-income communities.

Thrive outlined 16 objectives and called for completing 59 related actions by 2025 – from requiring green building standards for new construction, expanding green space, and reducing fossil-fuel use in the energy grid, to supporting "living wages" and reducing food insecurity. In 2017, Mayor Joe Hogsett pledged the city would reach carbon neutrality for the community by 2050, and Thrive set a goal of powering municipal operations completely via renewable energy sources by 2028.

Before those efforts could begin, the pandemic struck. In May 2020, downtown racial justice protests sparked by the police shooting of twenty-one-year-old Dreasjon Reed devolved into riots that left two dead, scores injured by police tear-gas, and more than 100 people arrested over a single weekend.[17] Like in other cities, homicides skyrocketed throughout 2020 after the pandemic,

---

[17] www.indystar.com/story/news/local/indianapolis/2021/05/28/indianapolis-riots-and-protests-looking-back-one-year-later/7478725002/

and minority communities disproportionately bore the economic and health consequences of the pandemic (Deslatte, Hatch, and Stokan 2020).

> The resilience of our neighborhoods – especially our Black and Brown communities, and our most vulnerable communities – have been shown to be exactly that," said one interviewee. "They had to work; they didn't have the opportunity to stay home. ... And thus they disproportionately were affected by COVID and disproportionately passed away because of that. And it disproportionately affected their income. Like, all those things have just been proven. That's a big thing for our office to try to tackle with a sustainability plan."

The performance management literature often conceptualizes performance outcomes as the end-result of some organizational implementation process. But in urban sustainability – a point exacerbated by the pandemic – outcomes are often a starting point for design processes. In many cases, public managers are wading into interconnected consequences from decades-long social, environmental, and economic disinvestments and injustices. In this sense, altering outcomes requires understanding their root causes, but also the limits of local government authority to directly or quickly impact many of them.

Indianapolis has a long history of racial and environmental injustices. Thrive noted that communities of color have a 66% higher rate of exposure to air pollution than predominantly white neighborhoods. The city had far less access to green space and public lands than the national average, crumbling infrastructure in low-income communities, and one of the lowest recycling rates in the country.[18] Among major-league cities, Indianapolis frequently ranked among the worst in mass transit investments and availability.

Acknowledging these challenges, Thrive focused on sustainability through an equity lens and was designed with performance management in mind. Associated with its fifty-nine action items, the document laid out nine "output metrics," to be reported on annually, and twenty "performance metrics," which would be reported on every three years. Among the annual output metrics, the Indianapolis Office of Sustainability (OoS) would begin tracking the number of "green buildings" constructed to either LEED certification levels or Energy Star ratings. It would track the number of building owners reporting their energy use and the number of EV vehicles sales and charging stations installed citywide. On the social front, the office was tasked with determining how many "large corporations" in the city paid "family-sustaining" wages to workers, the number of youths participating in after-school and summer recreational programs, and the percentage of residents with health insurance. Finally, the miles of bike lanes

---

[18] www.indystar.com/story/news/environment/2019/01/30/indianapolis-biggest-city-u-s-without-recycling-all/1272400002/

would be tracked along with the total tonnage of recycled trash. For each of these output metrics, a numerical goal was established for 2025. Many of these measurement efforts would require institutional changes to incentivize reporting new types of data.

However, the large number of indicators and benchmarks also presented a complicated mosaic of successes and challenges. City planners identified a host of economic, health, and environmental metrics to track, such as the percentage of children living in food insecurity, increasing housing prices, rising obesity rates, and the presence of "food deserts" where lower-income residents must travel miles for groceries. Many of the metrics in the plan were the product of slow-moving, unclear, or complex causal mechanisms and were difficult for the city to influence through policies or programs. While the city made strides in implementing its plan during the pandemic, managers also struggled to identify ways to measure some desired outcomes and to make sense of the performance measurements they were generating. This required consistent reengagement with key stakeholders to reassess metrics and even foundational definitions used in the report.

> "Taking stock of where we're at with those annual indicators is just as important as the bigger goals," said one interviewee. "And it brings to light maybe new things that weren't captured by the original plan. But also having that conversation with our community is important."

The Indianapolis experience illustrated a design process called *outcome identification*, whereby managers collected performance metrics that conform to organizational goals, made sense of confounding or contradictory results, and framed performance to keep partners engaged and supportive of the objectives. These three heuristic-based subroutines correspond with a nascent performance management literature in sustainability (Deslatte 2019; Park and Krause 2020; Opp, Mosier, and Osgood 2018). Performance management can be challenging due to the highly contextualized nature of city sustainability efforts (Deslatte 2020b), the need to constantly refine the vision for what sustainability efforts can accomplish (Elgert 2018), and the necessity to frame gains and losses to the public and elected officials in ways that maintain or build support (Park and Krause 2020). This design process features managers grappling with the reality that sustainability-related outcomes are ubiquitous. In an increasingly complex stream of data and communication frames, managers must identify causes and consequences of organizational actions that are influencing these outcomes and then make the case for maintaining, strengthening, or diverting organizational focus. This leads to the final proposition:

Proposition 3: *Outcome identification is a necessary but not sufficient condition to institutionalize sustainability performance gains.*

Even in the twenty-first century, establishing causal relationships between governmental actions and outcomes tends to remain the currency of academic policy analysis and program evaluation communities. Local governments rarely have the capabilities to identify causal linkages statistically and must interpret data from a single case (often, their own) in an intuitive or narrative fashion (Park and Krause 2020). They do so in order to make claims that strategies, policies or programs are leading to measured progress as well as to lobby for new resources or policies (Belardinelli et al. 2018).

The remainder of this section is focused on the difficulties dealing with performance outcomes in Indianapolis. The analysis inductively identified and assessed three heuristic-based subroutines: *measuring*, *updating*, and *framing*. Depicted in Figure 5, these subroutines involve collecting available performance indicators corresponding to ongoing social, economic, or environmental phenomena, evaluating outcomes based on either consistent or inconsistent decision rules for determining success, and selectively presenting them in ways that emphasize some characteristics and deemphasize others.

The evidence comes from planning documents and internal reports, media coverage, recordings of the Indianapolis City-County Commission on Environmental Sustainability and other legislative meetings, budget data and participant interviews. Table 3 reports the actors, activities and evidence types.

Outcome Identification

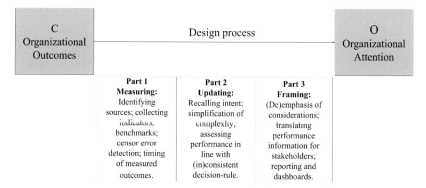

Figure 5 Depicts outcome identification as comprising measuring via indicators and benchmarks, sensemaking in the face of complexity, and framing as performance is translated for stakeholders and certain considerations are emphasized over others. These actions occur iteratively or intermittently as implementation efforts are evaluated.

Table 3 Heuristic subroutines of outcome identification

	Measuring	Updating	Framing
Actors	Sustainability staff; consultants; stakeholders.	Advisory boards; policymakers; sustainability staff; advocates.	Elected officials; Sustainability staff; stakeholders.
Activities	Data source identification and collection; error detection.	Recalling intent; dialogue facilitating social construction of problems, solutions.	Weighting of specific sustainability considerations (i.e. cost savings) over others.
Empirical fingerprint	Performance reports.	Forums where purpose, intent of organizational strategy are discussed.	Substantive emphasis on costs/ benefits of specific sustainability considerations in reports, media.
Evidence type	Pattern; account.	Sequence; pattern; account.	Trace; account.
Theoretical certainty	High	Low	High
Uniqueness	Low	High	Low

Measuring

Measuring is a subroutine that involves collecting, analyzing, and reporting data on the activities, outputs, or outcomes related to an organization's mission and goals (Moynihan and Pandey 2010; Van Dooren and Van de Walle 2016). Measuring is an obvious necessity for identifying the causes and consequences of government action. But, the adage that one cannot "manage what they do not measure" also blurs the reality that performance information presents a grainy snapshot of reality and can be used to advance political or "perverse" purposes (Moynihan and Pandey 2010).

Originating from the private sector, where measures of production and profitability are more readily available (Ghalayini and Noble 1996), performance measurement has become synonymous with the New Public Management. Reforms launched in the 1990s often mandated performance reporting in US federal agencies (Lynch and Day 1996). The underlying assumption of performance measurement and management is that harvesting data and comparing performance outcomes to some agreed-to standards would help governments make more efficient resource decisions (Kravchuk and Schack 1996; Moynihan and Lavertu 2012). Public administration scholars have long pushed back on this assumption, pointing out the prevalence of goal conflicts, questions about democratic accountability and the complexity embedded within public organizational missions and objectives (Moynihan 2008; Radin 2006). For instance, a recent meta-analysis of thirty-one strategic planning studies found evidence that planning-performance linkages are stronger when effectiveness – rather than efficiency – is the evaluative criterion for performance (George, Walker, and Monster 2019). While performance metrics may appear technical and value-neutral, they are often laden with assumptions and political values reflecting normative views of the worth of social benefits (Tilbury 2004).

Recent evidence within behavioral public administration has also highlighted the biases managers, citizens, and elected officials display when they interpret performance information (Belardinelli et al. 2018; Bellé, Cantarelli, and Belardinelli 2017; George, Baekgaard, and Decramer 2018; Jilke 2018; Meier et al. 2015; Van Dooren and Van de Walle 2016). This work has generally found a negativity bias in how citizens (James and John 2007; James and Moseley 2014; Olsen 2015) and politicians (Nielsen and Moynihan 2017) interpret public-sector performance metrics.

Public managers also display various biases – such as loss aversion, anchoring, and status quo biases – when assessing their performance (Bellé, Cantarelli, and Belardinelli 2018; Bullock, Greer, and O'Toole 2019; Nicholson-Crotty, Nicholson-Crotty, and Webeck 2019). Loss aversion, for instance, has been shown to influence how managers assess the viability of launching new sustainability-related methane-capture initiatives (Deslatte, Swann, and Feiock 2020). A consensus within this literature is that public employees can draw subjective conclusions or misinterpret evidence of program or policy outcomes even when trying to make accurate assessments.

Along these lines, some scholars have drawn attention to the use of performance information by local governments (Ammons 2015; Andrews 2009; Wang 2002). Owing to their broad scope of implementation responsibilities and resource constraints, local governments have a need for performance information collection and use. However, evidence suggests that while cities have increasingly turned to performance measurement during the last two decades, most do not systematically link their planning activities to performance assessments and budgeting (Andrews and Boyne 2010; Poister 2010; Poister and Streib 1999). This can be attributed to an institutionally derived disconnect between planning time frames and the operational venues in which managers make decisions (Poister 2010). Strategic goals and objectives are developed intermittently and can be shelved when information on progress is lacking or disconnected from the routines of managers. This is why the IAD focuses on the "evaluation" of outcomes that result from the choices made by actors in interactive situations.

To date, local sustainability researchers have devoted scant attention to how performance information is used. For instance, cities striving to reduce GHG emissions collect performance information infrequently and inconsistently (Krause et al. 2019). Lacking a standard framework for identifying and measuring sustainability, recent survey evidence suggests a majority of larger US cities do collect some form of performance information on their efforts, but use it less consistently to make decisions, communicate to stakeholders, or enhance programs (Park and Krause 2020).

While some evidence suggests that US sustainability measurement efforts within the last decade have led to performance gains (Deslatte and Swann 2020), this is largely based on the perceptions of program managers rather than objective information. Moreover, experimental evidence paints a more circumspect portrait of the value of sustainability performance measurement. It suggests citizens display both negativity bias (Deslatte 2020b) and partisan motivated reasoning (Deslatte 2019) when assessing social sustainability efforts such as energy-efficiency improvements in affordable housing. Risk aversion can also set in when public managers assess their own sustainability performance – leading them to avoid expanding efforts if performance is just meeting expectations (Deslatte, Swann, and Feiock 2020). While measuring sustainability performance may be gaining traction, the lack of consistent standards and guidance create conditions for subjective interpretation and misuse.

Indianapolis found itself in this predicament when it began attempting to implement Thrive. The plan was crafted through collaboration with nine consulting firms, fifteen local government agencies and more than two dozen community groups. Following its 2019 release, Indianapolis' OoS director resigned and the position went unfilled throughout 2020. By the time a new director was installed, the city had lost some momentum due to the pandemic and a hiring freeze, while its staff struggled to make sense of performance metrics largely developed by consultants and previous staffers.

Sustainability scholars have noted some performance metrics play a more "headline-grabbing" role while other technical indicators or benchmarks may be useful for internal management but less so for external legitimacy-seeking (Ji and Darnall 2018; Niemann and Hoppe 2018; Opp, Mosier, and Osgood 2018). Thrive attempted to strike some balance between these information types, although it ultimately offered less-then-desired guidance for the performance-minded staffers tasked with implementation.

> "You need to understand the metrics that we're going to be measuring to determine if the needle's moving forward," said one interviewee. "Ideally, the action items should be moving the metrics."

Two overarching measurement problems emerged in 2020. First, the plan's metrics were fuzzy. Many of the actions slated through 2025 were attached to open-ended goals without benchmarks or clear numeric targets, such as "increasing transit-oriented development," "encourag[ing] local businesses" to adopt alternative commuting incentives, or "increas[ing] green spaces to improve storm-water filtration." Without knowing the starting point or goal for such increases, it was impossible to create a decision rule for determining success or failure.

Staff also lacked a data dictionary or metadata repository for recreating measurements and identifying data origins, usage, and formatting. For instance, Thrive set a goal of installing 300 Electric Vehicle (EV) charging stations by 2025. When the OoS attempted to verify the number of EV charging stations throughout the city a year after plan adoption, they discovered the number had decreased from the recorded baseline of 170 to 152, even as electric vehicle sales were increasing. Digging deeper, they were unable to determine which data sources were used to establish Thrive's baseline. The original data may have been collected from publicly available commercial apps that drivers could use to locate EV stations; but, the staff struggled with determining why the number decreased from year to year.

> "In reality, some may have been over-counted in 2018. It's hard to say. And some of those stations may have been discontinued because of potentially a lack of use," said one interviewee. "There could be a wide variety of reasons why the numbers are different."

With no clear framework for measuring performance coupled with the expectation for annual performance reporting requirements, the sustainability office struggled to understand the data that went into establishing baselines for each metric:

> "We essentially had to reverse-engineer the output metrics that we were supposed to report on," said one interviewee.

A second problem arose from the expansiveness of Thrive's goals. Essentially, being more inclusive and incorporating community or environmental goals from a wide range of stakeholders can increase the difficulty measuring progress. Strategic planning research has found that increased participation in planning may weaken the relationship between planning and performance outcomes (George, Walker, and Monster 2019). The more comprehensive the planning, the more difficult performance measurement becomes because the desired outcomes increase. Thrive included goals intended to encourage employers to offer "family-sustaining wages" without clear guidance for how the local government could create such incentives or even how to quantify what a minimal level of "family-sustaining" income should be. It also set goals for creating "green jobs" initiatives and coworking spaces without defining these terms or what they would look like. Moreover, information on which stakeholder had originally proposed the goals was also lacking.

> "We just heard a lot of feedback and then our consultants … tried to synthesize exactly what was heard, not necessarily considering execution, feasibility, or implementation," said one interviewee.

Some of the clearer, performance-oriented components of the plan came with ready-made metrics and software. For instance, a primary focus of the office following the pandemic was to seek city adoption of an energy benchmarking and reporting ordinance for commercial buildings. While 66% of the community's GHG emissions came from buildings in 2016, Indianapolis had lagged behind surrounding peer cities such as St. Louis, Minneapolis, or Columbus, Ohio, in adopting any building energy usage and reporting requirements. The adoption of an energy benchmarking and transparency policy was also a top goal within Thrive's built environment recommendations and a key area of emphasis for the Bloomberg Philanthropies' ACCC effort. The city formed a Building Efficiency Advisory Committee of large building owners, utilities, and other community groups, which met throughout 2020.

The selling point for benchmarking policies was that they increased awareness of energy or water use on properties for both owners and potential renters of building spaces. Many building owners/operators choose to make improvements voluntarily when they realize doing so will cut down on utility bills. City consultants had determined that a benchmarking ordinance could eventually save owners and residents $16 million annually, achieve a 26% emissions reduction as well as creating green jobs and public health savings. Administratively, the EPA's Energy Star Portfolio Manager software was already a widely used platform for standardizing the tracking and reporting of energy use across various sizes and types of buildings.

Ultimately, the Indianapolis City-County Council adopted a version of the ordinance in mid-2021, which required city buildings to begin reporting energy and water use in 2022 with commercial and multifamily buildings over 50,000-square-feet to follow by 2024. The approach was less stringent than in other cities in that it exempted manufacturing and industrial properties and did not set goals for reducing energy use. However, it reflected an attempt to institutionalize the reporting and measuring of energy-use outcomes, tailored to local community norms:

> "We're Indianapolis. We're not Seattle or San Diego," Abbey Brands, the city's deputy director for planning and policy in the Department of Public Works, told lawmakers.

In summary, there is circumstantial evidence that performance measurement facilitated the identification of outcomes in a useful way for focusing public attention. Managers were aware and concerned about measurement difficulties. However, because performance measurement can serve cross-purposes, the theoretical uniqueness of measuring is low. As mentioned, the sustainability literature notes that local governments often engage in initial performance reporting efforts as a means for seeking external legitimacy rather than managing performance (Niemann and Hoppe 2018). It is also theoretically possible that election-motivated credit-claiming and career advancement can explain why policymakers, advocates, and even sustainability managers focus on specific metrics. This can lead to the expedient or strategic selection of some forms of information and the omission of others. Thus, an important managerial subroutine that can help to distinguish between these motivations is updating beliefs about the observed phenomena.

Updating

Updating is the management-supported subroutine of rationalizing experiences in ways that continue to motivate organizational action. It is derived from the Bayesian updating from cognitive science wherein individual beliefs or attitudes color interpretation of new information. Individuals update their beliefs when they encounter new, often conflicting information. But at an organizational level, updating alludes to a stream of organizational literature called sensemaking, which is focused on socially constructing a problem in a way that facilitates organizational identity and action (Audette-Chapdelaine 2016; Weick 1995).

Sensemaking theory, largely originating with Karl Weick (2015), argues that organizations try to make sense of events through a process of recognizing the chaos of current conditions, bracketing and labeling components of a stream of experiences, then making both retrospective judgments about the origins of these observations and presumptions to guide future actions. Similarly, updating here refers to an iterative cognitive and communicative effort of orienting the organization to changing conditions by searching for meaning and constructing a plausible "narrative" that restores normalcy and purpose to organizational life. For a time, it makes the world make sense again and animates organizational missions.

Indianapolis policymakers and managers engaged in updating in the wake of the pandemic's disparate impact on minority communities. As the local economy shuttered, lower-income and largely minority households were disproportionately forced to risk their lives going to work in-person and suffered greater economic consequences from the shutdown. Against this backdrop, Indianapolis policymakers and sustainability managers were tasked with reviewing how to implement Thrive. As they did so, they reevaluated their manner of engagement with disadvantaged communities along with the plan's language of vulnerability and resilience.

Updating is a product of the often-biased narrative nature of human cognition. It entails taking notice of ecological change or disruption within a constant stream of ordinary experience. To resolve the disruption, actors attempt to isolate or "bracket" components of the phenomenon from the continuous flow of experiences (Weick, Sutcliffe, and Obstfeld 2005). They then label and classify these bracketed observations, retroactively assessing what actions or mistakes created them (Weick 1995). Because time is fleeting, action is taken concurrently with discussion about the problem. Eventually, individual beliefs evolve into a shared understanding of the problem, based on presumptions about the future. A key here is that actions often precede collective decisions or judgments. At the organizational level, updating is driven by the need to socially construct plausible explanations for the disruptions, normalize them within the broader stream of experiences, and allow organizational efforts to continue.

Sequence and account evidence for updating was drawn from the 2020 meetings of a City-County Council study commission on environmental sustainability. The commission found itself in the midst of the pandemic deliberating how to reconcile the objectives of Thrive with longstanding inequities within the city's older, predominantly Black neighborhoods. During the meetings, environmental justice advocates detailed how construction of Interstates 65 and 70 to the east of downtown in the 1960s had carved up the historically Black neighborhood of Martindale Brightwood, separating homes from schools and parks and leading to a slow out-migration of higher-income residents and businesses.

Advocates noted that environmental problems remain prevalent in the community today. The soil that homeowners used to grow vegetables is heavily lead-contaminated. While comprising only 1% of the county's total land-area, the neighborhood today fields 12% of the service calls for illegal dumping. Its past land uses, allowing industrial facilities to be sited next to homes and churches, continue to haunt its present, with fifty-eight abandoned commercial or industrial sites potentially leaching pollution into the ground and water and dozens more that could become problems.

> "We are angry that our civil rights continue to be violated because we are an older, African American community," Elizabeth Gore, the chair of the Martindale Brightwood Environmental Justice Collaborative, told the commission in one hearing in summer 2020. "We feel that this industrial behavior would not be tolerated in more affluent neighborhoods, and we just feel it shouldn't be tolerated here."

During Thrive's planning, the city staff and consultants had conducted a seven-month community outreach where the city's "Street Team" attended over 150 community events, collected 3,152 survey responses, and engaged in substantial social media and online interactions, resulting in "contacts" with more than 265,000 Indianapolis residents. However, community members noted that efforts targeting minority neighborhoods were often led by outsiders without specific knowledge of the communities. While numerous groups have been active within the community, the root causes – the historic disinvestment and power imbalances – are largely unseen and unaddressed.

> "The stakeholders have good intentions, but I felt that they don't really know that community," said Paula Brooks, Environmental Health Senior Advisor with the Hoosier Environmental Council. "Generations have been overburdened and also engaged and nothing's happened ... There's a lack of trust between the community and the stakeholder organizations seeking to make improvements."

One culminating product of this engagement was Thrive's focus on social vulnerability: a spatial snapshot of areas of the city with greater concentrations of populations more at-risk to high temperatures and flooding, based on factors such as the densities of low-income, elderly, seniors, renters, the disabled, SNAP (food stamp) recipients, limited-English speakers, and those who identified as non-white. The plan noted that while these factors do not make a person "inherently vulnerable," the use of the term was an acknowledgment of "the system's deficiencies rather than as a judgment of any particular community members or neighborhoods."

The social vulnerability index (SVI) – modeled after the US Centers for Disease Control and Prevention's metric for assessing vulnerability to disease outbreaks – allowed the Thrive team to develop maps that showed how more vulnerable neighborhoods in the city could be disproportionately impacted by flooding and high-heat in the future.

> "A document like this did not exist for the City of Indianapolis before Thrive," the city's former sustainability director, Katie Robinson, told the commission at its inaugural meeting in 2020.

While the tool had been used to identify Martindale Brightwood as a location for a future resilience hub to distribute food, provide services, and provide heating and cooling stations, the abstract nature of the term prompted some reflection. Advocates, for instance, questioned whether the use of the term "vulnerability" washed over the root causes of environmental injustices.

> "You can talk about vulnerabilities in the abstract and maybe the community understands what vulnerabilities are in the abstract, maybe they don't. But they absolutely do understand when you talk about what environmental injustice is," said Commissioner Keith Veal, a sustainability and community development executive. "If we can be open and honest and call environmental injustice what it is – and call environmental justice a goal to be achieved – then we can better deal with the challenge of meeting short-term needs and long-term desires. Those don't have to be competing interests."

Throughout the hearings, Indianapolis policymakers and staff deliberated on concepts like equity and vulnerability and what that should mean for allocating resources and assessing progress. Thrive's climate action and sustainability goals – while developed through the lens of equity – were reevaluated to consider express racial inequities and remedies:

> "We're not saving our planet; we're saving ourselves, and it has to be all of us," one interviewee said in explaining how mindsets had changed after 2020. "It can't just be some of us who work for it and benefit from it."

These deliberations may have influenced subsequent decisions. The commission ultimately recommended – and the Indianapolis City-County Council later approved – a transit-oriented development ordinance to drive denser development and affordable housing along key transit corridors and future rapid-bus routes. In 2021, Mayor Hogsett announced the city would spend $20 million to build a new community center in the Frederick Douglass Park in Martindale

Brightwood. A standing City-County Council environmental sustainability committee was also created and began meeting in 2022, an institutional arrangement intended in part to give greater voice to environmental justice issues.

In summary, there is evidence that policymakers and managers engaged in updating to explain and justify future organizational actions. In interviews, sustainability staff indicated that the experiences of 2020 reenforced for them the importance of staying visible and "continuing to tell the story." Doing so involves the heuristic-based subroutine of framing outcomes in ways that support continued investment and action.

Framing

Framing is the act of emphasizing specific considerations about an issue in ways that resonate with audiences, the public, or policymakers. Originating in psychology, political science, and behavioral economics, framing theory attempts to understand how the weighting of specific dimensions of policies or issues by a messenger can tap into distinct considerations or values on the part of the receiver (Chong and Druckman 2007a; Druckman, Fein, and Leeper 2012).

Known as *issue framing*, this occurs when one or more of several substantively distinct considerations surrounding a policy issue are raised (Chong and Druckman 2007b; Deslatte 2020c; Druckman 2001; Gross 2008; Kahneman and Tversky 1986; Slothuus 2008). The framing literature defines this as an *emphasis frame*, which highlights specific features of a policy or event and ignores or minimizes others. *Framing effects* can result when emphasis frames lead the recipient to access relevant memories, leading to either a strengthening or weakening of prior attitudes or beliefs (Oxley 2020). Framing effect studies have typically focused on campaign messaging, elite mobilization, and political party competition (Druckman 2004; Slothuus and de Vreese 2010), while the outcomes they consider range from respondents' concern about an issue to their behavioral intent and support for government policies.

Framing efforts are crucial for sustainability, given the multidimensional nature of its social, economic and environmental objectives. For instance, one study on the influence of competing issue frames surrounding a local government growth management initiative – that it would preserve green space but impose economic costs – found that citizen exposure to either the strong "pro" or "con" frames via editorials significantly swayed support above or below the mean, respectively (Chong and Druckman 2007b). Research has examined Republicans' resistance to accepting the scientific consensus on anthropogenic climate change, which has implications for how to frame progress on sustainability initiatives (Bayes, Bolsen, and Druckman 2020; Bolsen and Druckman 2018).

During the pandemic lockdown, experimental evidence suggested that frames that emphasized economic recovery over public health positively influenced intent to engage in non-essential grocery shopping (Deslatte 2020c).

However, the conclusions that can be drawn from research on framing effects remain circumspect. Recent evidence suggests "strategic" issue frames do not influence meat-consumption and fossil-fuel vehicle use (Fesenfeld et al. 2021). Alternatively, some evidence suggests citizens may be more supportive of climate-policy investments when presented with positive performance frames (Deslatte 2020b). There is also conflicting evidence over the causal mechanisms at play in framing effects (Bayes, Bolsen, and Druckman 2020). For example, accessibility of memories, attitudes, or beliefs might play a role in how frame recipients respond, but so might partisan or social identities and consensus-seeking (Bayes and Druckman 2021) or psychological reactance – an oppositional response to perceived social pressure that can produce a "backfire" effect (Brehm and Brehm 2013; Ma, Dixon, and Hmielowski 2019).

Despite debate over the mechanisms and contexts in which they might prove effective, framing is ubiquitous in practice (Chong and Druckman 2007a; Tuchman 1978). Framing was evident as Indianapolis managers sought to promote a particular belief or attitude about Thrive's policy objectives and keep them on the institutional agenda. Within the process of outcome identification, framing is an externally directed act that links measuring and updating to the outcome of organizational attention.

In Indianapolis, the framing of sustainability initiatives and outcomes dates back to shortly after the formation of the OoS in 2008 and has evolved over the years. Formed under Republican mayor Greg Ballard, the OoS was initially tasked with advancing the mayor's goal to make the city more competitive for talented workers, officials said.

> "He saw it as kind of a way to encourage young people to stay here or to be pulled to Indianapolis because of the sustainability effort," said one interviewee. "He also saw cost savings in some of the stuff."

This is evidenced in the office's annual progress reports issued from 2008–2012, which emphasized green-infrastructure initiatives like rain gardens, the expansion of bike-lanes across the city, waste-water cleanup efforts, and recycling. As then-mayor Ballard wrote in the 2010 report, a focus on sustainability would "create a community that is more livable and safer for those who live and work here," and "foster sustainable growth, making ours a more attractive place for economic progress." Objectives such as climate action and social equity were not emphasized in these early reports.

By 2019, the issue-framing emphasis had shifted to consider equity and climate. Thrive framed resilience by emphasizing the disparate heat, flooding, and health impacts of climate change on vulnerable populations. This frame was strengthened by policymakers' 2020 environmental justice deliberations.

In the 2021 Thrive progress report, the OoS director noted the pandemic had "upended our way of life and laser-focused our attention on the racism and inequality still prevalent in our society." The report argued that the lack of access to health care and employment opportunities "closely mirrors how climate change disproportionately burdens these communities and serves as a stark reminder that equitable action is more urgent than ever." The update moved beyond focusing on just the nine "output metrics" that were to be reported on annually and featured "nineteen related data points and stories demonstrating collective progress toward sustainability and resiliency."

These vignettes highlighted several social and community programs, including: a Pathways to Employment program for the homeless; the distribution of reusable face masks; the mayor's Project Indy youth jobs program; Indy Parks' summer and after-school programs; increased numbers of urban gardens and groceries that accept SNAP (food stamp) payments; and the city's Community Nutrition and Food Policy division created in 2021.

The report also noted that the percentage of Indianapolis residents with health insurance increased slightly during 2020, due to ongoing implementation of the federal Affordable Care Act. While the city was not responsible for this outcome, its inclusion in the report illustrates how "COVID actually created the conversation about the inequities in our society," one interviewee said.

The emphasis framing, interviewees noted, was intended to help draw attention to social and racial justice goals, as well as attempting to make a bipartisan case for resilience and sustainability investments as the plan's 2025 objectives draw closer.

> "Ultimately, it's about human life and how climate action is going to further benefit our day to day life," said one interviewee.

In summary, there is circumstantial evidence that framing facilitated outcome identification. While sustainability performance reporting can be utilized for internal management and policy decisions, the emphasis framing in Indianapolis appeared aimed at external legitimacy-seeking. The observed frames highlighted accomplishments as a means to build support among policymakers and stakeholders and leverage broader investments. This framing de-emphasized planned activities that had not yet begun, such as piloting a resilience hub or microgrid to increase resilience. It also placed less emphasis on green energy and more on social outcomes to foster an equity-focused narrative for maintaining political and financial support.

The Results of Outcome Identification

Outcome identification involves managing organizational attention. Throughout the pandemic, Indianapolis grappled with how to begin Thrive's implementation. City staff were challenged to determine how to measure and manage progress in the face of unclear planning goals and complex social outcomes. These outcomes were paradoxically a product of past governmental policies and disinvestment but also beyond the city's short-term control. Through the subroutines of measurement, updating, and framing, the city's sustainability staff sought to both refocus public and elite attention on its efforts and motivate Thrive's implementation through a lens of environmental justice and equity. The evidence indicates staff engaged in outcome identification with the acknowledgment that many social outcomes of interest were beyond the power of the city-county government to impact.

At the same time, staff face the same capacity limitations that plagued strategy development and capability codification in the previous cases. In particular, projects such as the resilience hub, a microgrid and green jobs incubator have been pushed back or handed off to other agencies, freeing staff to focus on other program implementation. This reflects adaptation as conditions or context change and resources are reallocated.

Outcome identification as a design process can help managers maintain momentum in implementation of their plans as well as make adjustments when conditions or circumstances change. It also plays a role in setting expectations when confronting limited resources and ambiguous goals. As one OoS staffer put it during a Thrive implementation meeting in 2020:

> Our team is relatively small, and there's 59 action items. And each one of those action items is a huge lift. So, I hope it is understandable that our team has not identified the exact resource that would fit each of those action items and gotten it to stage H of an entire alphabet.

Over the course of two years, Indianapolis policymakers and sustainability managers created a hybrid performance framework emphasizing both outcomes they can control (e.g. the number of EV charging stations, mileage of bike paths, and green infrastructure projects) alongside those that are broader societal problems but that illustrate or frame key equity considerations (e.g. the lack of health care, unemployment, or food deserts).

At the same time, Indianapolis ended 2021 by enacting several notable institutional arrangements that could facilitate the routinization of performance information use and future strategy adjustments. These include the creation of a full-time standing City-County Council Environmental Sustainability Committee, which began monitoring Thrive implementation progress in 2022, and the passage of building energy benchmarking and transit-oriented development ordinances to track energy performance and investments in the community's built environment for years to come.

Outcome identification that links organizational performance to attention and adjustment is a critical but little-understood design process in local sustainability. An expanding literature on behavioral public administration has focused on various means of "nudging" citizen attitudes and behavioral intent (Battaglio et al. 2019; Vlaev et al. 2016), but theory and evidence for guiding managers and policymakers on the use of sustainability and climate-related performance information remains sparse. Framing of performance information is likely to take on greater practical and scholarly importance as both local government policymakers and public administrators seek to advance sustainability and climate-action goals in the near term (Deslatte, Swann, and Feiock 2020; Park and Krause 2020).

5 Institutionalizing Design Processes: Challenges and Future Directions for Managing City Sustainability

Cities are complex, adaptive systems. Outcomes that are observed in such systems are the progeny of many causal mechanisms. The strategic management literature on public organizations has found that both strategy content and environmental contingencies can impact local government performance (George, Walker, and Monster 2019). But this literature tends to "black box" the processes that connect environmental contexts to the production of strategies, their effectuation, and evaluation.

This Element theorized and empirically examined sustainability efforts through three heuristic-based design processes. Strategy assemblage, capability codification, and outcome identification were deductively developed, and then nine heuristic-based subroutines or activities were inductively identified within these processes. These are inherently trial-and-error processes guided by the normative judgments and goals of humans. Cities define sustainability for themselves when they develop and update strategy goals. They animate sustainability progress through the refinement and abandonment of organizational capabilities. And they witness sustainability gains (or the lack thereof) via the collection, interpretation, and use of performance information in decision-making.

The analysis yielded several insights but was intended to raise more questions. Some of these design processes appeared to flow seamlessly into others in two cases (Bloomington and Indianapolis), while getting stymied in another (South Bend). But all three cases displayed stops and starts at different junctures. Across the cases, any single design process has the potential to produce errors, halting progress, and be abandoned. Nor can any single design process explain why sustainability progress is maintained. This illustrates the "disconnect" between planning and performance long noted in the public administration literature (Poister 2010). Moving forward, future research can further unpack these conceptual boxes to isolate specific mechanisms and their joint effects within these processes. But scholars must also make an effort to better understand how these processes become more-or-less integrated.

Understanding such integration requires greater attention to the system dynamics (information, material, and resource flows) influenced by these design processes (managing strategies, capabilities, and performance) under alternative institutional arrangements. Each process and heuristic-based subroutine is an activity aimed at learning and adaptation. They involve trial-and-error methods for reallocating resource flows. Meanwhile, institutions are the guideposts for human interactions within and between organizations, and they influence who gets to make decisions, who is impacted by them, and what rewards or sanctions exist to guide behavior (Ostrom 2011). Across the cases, the design processes made mostly incremental changes in resource flows, reflecting the risk entailed in realigning capabilities. Occasionally, the organizations formalized new responsibilities and resource commitments via formal institutional rules.

The evidence also suggests a broader possibility about institutionalization: that while the design processes and the heuristic-based subroutines may begin in sequential fashion under predetermined rules, they alter their institutional structure via cycles of iterative interaction. The IAD framework depicts cycles of patterned interaction as the fast feedback within action situations, and Figure 6 attempts to depict how iterations of our design processes may ultimately become more integrated.

Strategies may be developed, updated, and activated iteratively. Capabilities may be aligned and realigned. Performance metrics may change, or the same metrics may be reinterpreted and reframed. As the processes become more overlapping, integrating specific subroutines increases the odds of "sustaining sustainability" (Wang et al. 2012). Figure 6 illustrates how specific subroutines could hypothetically become more integrated over time. As integration occurs, the processes may gain a kind of centrifugal force that maintains momentum. The key will be developing nested models of the functional forms between subroutines, which can be empirically tested. For instance, this may rely on "inward" versus "outward" management

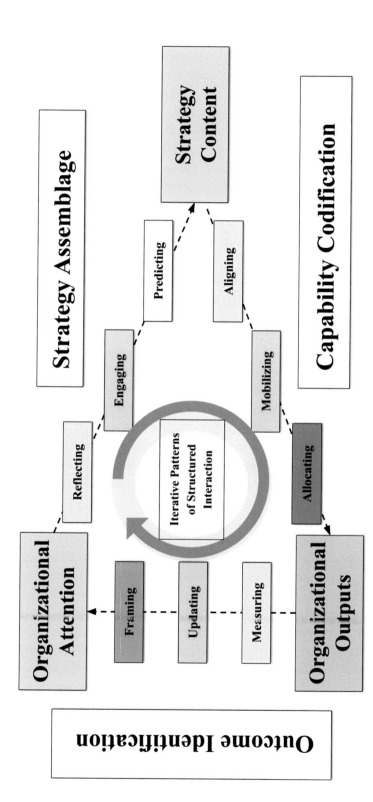

Figure 6 Displays potential hypotheses for how design processes and their management-led subroutines may integrate over cycles of iterative action. The color coding indicates subroutines that may integrate via feedback loops, or cyclical patterns of interaction and evaluation

orientations (O'Toole and Meier, 1999). Measuring outputs, reflecting on conditions, and aligning routines are each inward-focused management activities that may become more informally institutionalized. For instance, as Bloomington was assessing the performance of its solar pilot programs in 2021, policymakers were continuing to debate whether the city was making adequate climate-action progress and considering the merits of realigning sustainability staffing. As managers there acknowledged, some of the strategic goals and hundreds of related actions identified in their SAP/CAP may ultimately be abandoned as conditions change.

Conversely, updating, engaging, and mobilizing are outward-focused activities aimed at creating shared understanding with stakeholders, clients, and partners. In 2022, South Bend's new sustainability director was engaging with stakeholders in preparation to revise the city's climate-action and comprehensive plans, while concurrently working to mobilize community resources to implement solar and green building initiatives from the original CAP.

Meanwhile, predicting potential futures, framing performance information, and allocating resources are activities where managers play a supporting role to policymakers but also attempt to guide, inform, and steer their decisions. These subroutines may work on incongruous time scales (framing may occur every year, with predicting occurring less frequently during planning processes). But they all play an important role in adjacent subroutines. As cities continue implementing strategies, they may rely on updating and framing to "activate" strategies, mobilize partners, and allocate resources. In 2022, Indianapolis was laying the groundwork for collecting and assessing new performance information generated from its energy benchmarking ordinance for government and commercial buildings – named the "Thriving Buildings" program. Ostensibly, the data collected will help incentivize building owners to make energy-efficiency upgrades, but this will need to involve iteratively ramping-up resources devoted to data collection, framing, and dissemination in the community and to policymakers. Updating and framing here could impact the engagement, mobilization, and allocation of resources.

It is important to reiterate here that these processes are cyclical, produce changes via feedback, and can break down in multiple places. Integrating these design processes can increase the probability that strategy content will guide the development of capabilities, and that performance information-processing will allow managers to adapt. Integrating these processes may theoretically allow managers to adapt to unexpected outcomes. However, there are also likely many ways in which various management activities may be maladapted, overlooked, or executed in perfunctory and tokenistic fashion. While extant research has studied many of these elements in isolation – and there is need for more attention to each – there has not been a consistent effort to examine how these processes and subroutines interact over time.

For instance, evidence suggests staff support is important for embedding sustainability goals in strategic plans (Hawkins, Krause, and Deslatte 2021). Despite the pandemic, more than thirty municipalities in Indiana had either developed climate action plans (CAPs) or started the process of developing strategies by conducting municipal or community-wide greenhouse-gas inventories by 2022. But we have little empirical evidence about how such planning relates to capability development or performance outcomes.

Across all three design processes and nine subroutines, capabilities were critical. The capacity-building literature has suggested that all forms of political, administrative, fiscal, and technical "capacities" are important drivers of organizational innovation or action. But this research often simultaneously manages to blur mechanisms and ignore processes, resulting in little causal understanding or prescriptive guidance. This study has aimed to provide a framework for developing a resource-based theory of public organizational capabilities (Deslatte and Stokan 2020). Such a theory would allow us to more fruitfully distinguish contextual conditions from mechanisms within individual processes; posit causal relationships between subsets of these factors within or across these processes; and specify models with functional relationships between variables to test hypotheses (McGinnis 2011).

In summary, public administration scholars have long recognized the importance of linking strategic planning and performance management (Bryson, Berry, and Yang 2010; Moynihan and Pandey 2010; Park and Krause 2020; Poister 2010; Wang et al. 2012). An enduring criticism is that these processes are often rooted in the conceptualization of a system as a static, stable world where compartmentalized managers deal with predictable, linear changes. This is not a realistic facsimile of the real world. System dynamics are typically non-linear, and slow-moving feedback can trigger sudden shocks (Anderies et al. 2013). Due to climate change, cities will have little choice but to adapt. They will have to make choices about which outputs of system performance should be robust to change despite variability to inputs (i.e. clean water availability), which should be "safe to fail" (i.e. resilient), and which should be enhanced (i.e. public safety, economic opportunity) to more sustainable states (Anderies, Barreteau, and Brady 2019; Muneepeerakul and Anderies 2017).

Sustainability has been called an important organizing animus for public administration research in the twenty-first century (Fiorino 2010). Local government managers and policymakers make sustainability gains through iterative adjustments of organizational capabilities but face significant institutional inertia in doing so. We can advance both social science and societal progress with greater attention to how managers and policymakers integrate strategies, capabilities, and performance information use.

Thanks to anthropogenic climate change, cities can expect increased frequency, severity, and spatial distribution of high temperatures and humidity (Mukherjee et al. 2021), increased flooding events (Tubridy, Scott, and Lennon 2021), greater spread of vector-borne diseases and pandemics (Tajudeen and Oladunjoye 2021), and sea-level rise (Griggs 2021). This is not a dilemma facing the planners and administrators of 2050. This was the summer of 2021. Climate change wreaked havoc globally, from western US wildfires blanketing the continent in haze, Siberian forest fires and heat waves, mudslides in India, and communities washed away in Germany, to subway riders trapped by torrential flooding in Zhengzhou, China. The COVID-19 pandemic experience is only one example of sustainability threats under the cumulative pressures of fast- and slow-moving system feedback (Deslatte 2020d; Gaynor and Wilson 2020). Larger shocks are ahead. Just like governments, public administration as a field will have to reckon with them.

Glossary

Aligning   The administrative or manager-led organization and sequencing of events and responsibilities necessary to accomplish an organization's goals.

Allocating   The commitment of fiscal and human resources toward new organizational pursuits.

Biophysical Conditions   All relevant aspects of the engineered-environmental system in which an organization operates.

Capability   An organization's high-level strategic management potential, which encompasses both competencies and their linked capacities.

Capability Codification   The design process that comprises the subroutines of aligning, mobilizing, and allocating. It involves sequencing of events and formalization of coordination mechanisms and partners across administrative and sectoral silos to achieve goals.

Capacity   The aggregate level of resources committed to a specific competency.

Community Attributes   All relevant aspects of social or cultural context within which an organization operates.

Competency   Either core (possessed by many) or distinctive (unique) skills, expertise, know-how, or experiences that allow managers to strategically enhance organizational performance or value

Design Process   Activities drawing on the entrepreneurial abilities of managers, such as ideation, coordination, and effectuating the creation of public value.

Engaging   The enlistment of stakeholders in decision-making who have knowledge of local contexts and personal stakes in negotiating successful outcomes.

Framing   The act of emphasizing specific considerations about an issue – and de-emphasizing others – in ways that resonate with audiences, the public, or policymakers.

IAD Framework   A systems approach to studying policy and management processes, in which inputs are processed by actors into outputs and outcomes, which are evaluated via feedback effects.

Measuring   Collecting and reporting data on the activities, outputs, or outcomes related to an organization's enterprise functions.

Mobilizing   Identifying partners within an organizational task environment and motivating or leveraging their participation in collaborative efforts.

Outcome Identification   The design process that comprises the subroutines of measuring, updating, and framing. The collection of performance indicator or benchmark data, updating beliefs or predictions based on this information (with consistent or inconsistent decision rules), and framing performance in ways that emphasize some considerations over others.

Predicting   The involvement of a smaller subset of specialists attempting to understand how an organization's context and capabilities relate to future conceptual outcomes or scenarios.

Reflecting   The purposeful examination of an organization's existing planning efforts, its missions, mandates, strengths, and weaknesses.

Rules In Use   All relevant elements of the formal and informal institutional context in which an organization operates.

Strategy Assemblage   The design process that comprises the subroutines of reflecting, engaging, and predicting. The assessment/review of internal conditions, identification of peer organizations from which to imitate solutions, and selective use of information to determine goals.

Updating   Rationalizing experiences in ways that continue to motivate organizational action. It is derived from the Bayesian updating from cognitive science when individual beliefs or attitudes color an individual's interpretation of new information.

Bibliography

Aken, Joan Ernst van, and Hans Berends. 2018. *Problem Solving in Organizations*. Cambridge University Press.

Alibašić, Haris. 2018. *Sustainability and Resilience Planning for Local Governments: The Quadruple Bottom Line Strategy*. Springer.

Ammons, David. 2015. "Getting Real about Performance Management." *Public Management*. November 12. https://icma.org/articles/pm-magazine/pm-article-getting-real-about-performance-management.

Anastasopoulos, L. Jason, and Andrew B. Whitford. 2018. "Machine Learning for Public Administration Research, With Application to Organizational Reputation." *Journal of Public Administration Research and Theory 29* (3): 491–510.

Anderies, John M., Olivier Barreteau, and Ute Brady. 2019. "Refining the Robustness of Social-Ecological Systems Framework for Comparative Analysis of Coastal System Adaptation to Global Change." *Regional Environmental Change 19* (7): 1891–908.

Anderies, John M., Marco Janssen, and Elinor Ostrom. 2004. "A Framework to Analyze the Robustness of Social-Ecological Systems from an Institutional Perspective." *Ecology and Society* 9 (1). https://doi.org/10.5751/ES-00610-090118.

Anderies, John M., Carl Folke, Brian Walker, and Elinor Ostrom. 2013. "Aligning Key Concepts for Global Change Policy: Robustness, Resilience, and Sustainability." *Ecology and Society 18* (2): Article 8. http://dx.doi.org/10.5751/ES-05178-180208.

Anderson, Christopher J., Jennifer Gooden, Patrick E. Guinan et al. 2015. *Climate in the Heartland: Historical Data and Future Projections for the Heartland Regional Network: Urban Sustainability Directors Network*. Urban Sustainability Directors Network. https://www.usdn.org/uploads/cms/documents/climate in the heartland report.pdf.

Andrews, Rhys. 2009. "Organizational Task Environments and Performance: An Empirical Analysis." *International Public Management Journal 12* (1): 1–23.

Andrews, Rhys, and George A. Boyne. 2010. "Capacity, Leadership, and Organizational Performance: Testing the Black Box Model of Public Management." *Public Administration Review 70* (3): 443–54.

Andrews, Rhys, Malcolm J. Beynon, and Aoife M. McDermott. 2016. "Organizational Capability in the Public Sector: A Configurational

Approach." *Journal of Public Administration Research and Theory 26* (2): 239–58.

Audette-Chapdelaine, Marianne. 2016. "Sensemaking and the Political–Administrative Interface: The Challenges of Strategically Steering and Managing a Local Public Service." *International Review of Administrative Sciences 82* (3): 454–71.

Baez, Bien, and Mitchel Y. Abolafia. 2002. "Bureaucratic Entrepreneurship and Institutional Change: A Sense-Making Approach." *Journal of Public Administration Research and Theory 12* (4): 525–52.

Bardach, Eugene. 2004. "The Extrapolation Problem: How Can We Learn from the Experience of Others?" *Journal of Policy Analysis and Management 23* (2): 205–20.

Barzelay, Michael. 2007. "Learning from Second-Hand Experience: Methodology for Extrapolation-Oriented Case Research." *Governance 20* (3): 521–43.

2019. *Public Management as a Design-Oriented Professional Discipline.* Edward Elgar Publishing.

Barzelay, Michael, and Fred Thompson. 2010. "Back to the Future: Making Public Administration a Design Science." *Public Administration Review 70*: s295–97.

Battaglio, R. Paul, Jr., Paolo Belardinelli, Nicola Bellé, and Paola Cantarelli. 2018. "Behavioral Public Administration *ad fontes*: A Synthesis of Research on Bounded Rationality, Cognitive Biases, and Nudging in Public Organizations." *Public Administration Review 79*: 304–20.

Bayes, Robin, and James N. Druckman. 2021. "Motivated Reasoning and Climate Change." *Current Opinion in Behavioral Sciences 42*: 27–35.

Bayes, Robin, Toby Bolsen, and James N. Druckman. 2020. "A Research Agenda for Climate Change Communication and Public Opinion: The Role of Scientific Consensus Messaging and Beyond." *Environmental Communication.* https://doi.org/10.1080/17524032.2020.1805343.

Beach, Derek, and Rasmus Brun Pedersen. 2019. *Process-Tracing Methods: Foundations and Guidelines.* University of Michigan Press.

Beach, Derek, and Jonas Gejl Kaas. 2020. "The Great Divides: Incommensurability, the Impossibility of Mixed-Methodology, and What to Do about It." *International Studies Review 22* (2): 214–35.

Becker, Gary S. 1983. "A Theory of Competition among Pressure Groups for Political Influence." *The Quarterly Journal of Economics 98* (3): 371–400.

Beer, Michael. 2009. "Sustain Organizational Performance through Continuous Learning, Change and Realignment." In Edwin A. Locke, ed., *Handbook of Principles of Organizational Behavior*, 2nd ed. John Wiley & Sons, 537–55.

Belardinelli, Paolo, Nicola Bellé, Mariafrancesca Sicilia, and Ileana Steccolini. 2018. "Framing Effects under Different Uses of Performance Information: An Experimental Study on Public Managers." *Public Administration Review 78* (6): 841–51.

Bellé, Nicola, Paola Cantarelli, and Paolo Belardinelli. 2017. "Cognitive Biases in Performance Appraisal: Experimental Evidence on Anchoring and Halo Effects With Public Sector Managers and Employees." *Review of Public Personnel Administration 37* (3): 275–94.

Bellé, Nicola, Paola Cantarelli, and Paolo Belardinelli. 2018. "Prospect Theory Goes Public: Experimental Evidence on Cognitive Biases in Public Policy and Management Decisions." *Public Administration Review 78* (6): 828–40.

Berry, Frances Stokes. 2001. "Using Strategic Planning to Manage Strategically in the Public Sector." *Public Administration and Public Policy 91*: 261–90.

Besanko, David, David Dranove, Mark Shanley, and Scott Schaefer. 2009. *Economics of Strategy*. John Wiley & Sons.

Bingham, LisaB., Tina Nabatchi, and Rosemary O'Leary. 2005. "The New Governance: Practices and Processes for Stakeholder and Citizen Participation in the Work of Government." *Public Administration Review 65* (5): 547–58.

Blomquist, William Andrew, Edella Schlager, and Tanya Heikkila. 2004. *Common Waters, Diverging Streams: Linking Institutions to Water Management in Arizona, California, and Colorado*. Resources for the Future.

Boin, Arjen, and Cynthia Renaud. 2013. "Orchestrating Joint Sensemaking across Government Levels: Challenges and Requirements for Crisis Leadership." *Journal of Leadership Studies 7* (3): 41–46.

Bolsen, Toby, and James N. Druckman. 2018. "Do Partisanship and Politicization Undermine the Impact of a Scientific Consensus Message about Climate Change?" *Group Processes & Intergroup Relations 21* (3): 389–402.

Bolsen, Toby, James N. Druckman, and Fay Lomax Cook. 2014. "The Influence of Partisan Motivated Reasoning on Public Opinion." *Political Behavior 36* (2): 235–62.

Bovaird, Tony. 2008. "Emergent Strategic Management and Planning Mechanisms in Complex Adaptive Systems." *Public Management Review 10* (3): 319–40.

Bowman, Ann O'M. 2017. "The State-Local Government(s) Conundrum: Power and Design." *The Journal of Politics 79* (4): 1119–29.

Boyne, George A., and Richard M. Walker. 2010. "Strategic Management and Public Service Performance: The Way Ahead." *Public Administration Review 70* (2010): s185–92.

Brehm, Sharon S., and Jack W. Brehm. 2013. *Psychological Reactance: A Theory of Freedom and Control*. Academic Press.

Bryson, John M. 2010. "The Future of Public and Nonprofit Strategic Planning in the United States." *Public Administration Review 70* (December): s255–67.

2016. "Strategic Planning and the Strategy Change Cycle." In David O. Renz and Robert D. Herman, eds., *The Jossey-Bass Handbook of Nonprofit Leadership and Management*. John Wiley & Sons, 240–73.

2018. *Strategic Planning for Public and Nonprofit Organizations: A Guide to Strengthening and Sustaining Organizational Achievement*. John Wiley & Sons.

Bryson, John M., and Bert George. 2020. "Strategic Management in Public Administration." In William R. Thompson, ed., *Oxford Research Encyclopedia of Politics*. https://oxfordre.com/politics/view/10.1093/acrefore/9780190228637.001.0001/acrefore-9780190228637-e-1396.

Bryson, John M., Fran Ackermann, and Colin Eden. 2007. "Putting the Resource-Based View of Strategy and Distinctive Competencies to Work in Public Organizations." *Public Administration Review 67* (4): 702–17.

Bryson, John M., Frances S. Berry, and Kaifeng Yang. 2010. "The State of Public Strategic Management Research: A Selective Literature Review and Set of Future Directions." *American Review of Public Administration 40* (5): 495–521.

Bullock, Justin B., Robert A. Greer, and Laurence J. O'Toole. 2019. "Managing Risks in Public Organizations: A Conceptual Foundation and Research Agenda." *Perspectives on Public Management and Governance 2* (1): 75–87.

Carr, Jered B. 2015. "What Have We Learned about the Performance of Council-Manager Government? A Review and Synthesis of the Research." *Public Administration Review 75* (5): 673–89.

Carr, Jered B., and Christopher V. Hawkins. 2013. "The Costs of Cooperation: What the Research Tells Us about Managing the Risks of Service Collaborations in the US." *State and Local Government Review 45* (4): 224–39.

Chong, Dennis, and James N. Druckman. 2007a. "Framing Theory." *Annual Review of Political Science 10* (1): 103–26.

2007b. "Framing Public Opinion in Competitive Democracies." *The American Political Science Review 101* (4): 637–55.

Collier, David. 2011. "Understanding Process Tracing." *PS: Political Science & Politics 44* (4): 823–30.

Constas, Helen. 1958. "Max Weber's Two Conceptions of Bureaucracy." *The American Journal of Sociology 63* (4): 400–9.

Cowan, Robin, and Dominique Foray. 1997. "The Economics of Codification and the Diffusion of Knowledge." *Industrial and Corporate Change 6* (3): 595–622.

Cowan, Robin, Paul A. David, and Dominique Foray. 2000. "The Explicit Economics of Knowledge Codification and Tacitness." *Industrial and Corporate Change 9* (2): 211–53.

Curley, Cali, and Peter Federman. 2020. "State Executive Orders: Nuance in Restrictions, Revealing Suspensions, and Decisions to Enforce." *Public Administration Review 80* (4): 623–28.

Denhardt, Robert B. 1985. "Strategic Planning in State and Local Government." *State & Local Government Review 17* (1): 174–79.

Deslatte, Aaron. 2015. "Municipal Charters." In Domonic A. Bearfield and Melvin J. Dubnick, eds., *Encyclopedia of Public Administration and Public Policy*. Routledge.

2018. "Managerial Friction and Land-Use Policy Punctuations in the Fragmented Metropolis." *Policy Studies Journal 48* (3): 700–26.

2019. "A Bayesian Approach for Behavioral Public Administration: Citizen Assessments of Local Government Sustainability Performance." *Journal of Behavioral Public Administration 2* (1): 1–12.

2020a. "Revisiting Bureaucratic Entrepreneurialism in the Age of Urban Austerity: Framing Issues, Taking Risks, and Building Collaborative Capacity." In Muhammad Naveed Iftikhar, Jonathan B. Justice, and David B. Audretsch, eds., *Urban Studies and Entrepreneurship*. Springer International Publishing, 143–59.

2020b. "Positivity and Negativity Dominance in Citizen Assessments of Intergovernmental Sustainability Performance." *Journal of Public Administration Research and Theory 30* (4): 563–78.

2020c. "To Shop or Shelter? Issue Framing Effects and Social-Distancing Preferences in the COVID-19 Pandemic." *Journal of Behavioral Public Administration 3* (1). https://doi.org/10.30636/jbpa.31.158.

2020d. "The Erosion of Trust During a Global Pandemic and How Public Administrators Should Counter It." *American Review of Public Administration 50* (6–7): 489–96.

2020e. Review of *Repowering Cities: Governing Climate Change Mitigation in New York City, Los Angeles, and Toronto*, by Sara Hughes. *Perspectives on Politics 18* (4): 1267–69.

Deslatte, Aaron, and Eric Stokan. 2017. "Hierarchies of Need in Sustainable Development: A Resource Dependence Approach for Local Governance." *Urban Affairs Review 55* (4): 1125–52.

2020. "Sustainability Synergies or Silos? The Opportunity Costs of Local Government Organizational Capabilities." *Public Administration Review* 80 (6): 1024–34.

Deslatte, Aaron, and William L. Swann. 2016. "Is the Price Right? Gauging the Marketplace for Local Sustainable Policy Tools." *Journal of Urban Affairs 38* (4): 581–96.

2017. "Context Matters: A Bayesian Analysis of How Organizational Environments Shape the Strategic Management of Sustainable Development." *Public Administration 95* (3): 807–24. https://doi.org/10.1111/padm.12330.

2020. "Elucidating the Linkages Between Entrepreneurial Orientation and Local Government Sustainability Performance." *American Review of Public Administration 50* (1): 92–109.

Deslatte, Aaron, Megan E. Hatch, and Eric Stokan. 2020. "How Can Local Governments Address Pandemic Inequities?" *Public Administration Review 80* (5): 827–31.

Deslatte, Aaron, William L. Swann, and Richard C. Feiock. 2017. "Three Sides of the Same Coin? A Bayesian Analysis of Strategic Management, Comprehensive Planning, and Inclusionary Values in Land Use." *Journal of Public Administration Research and Theory 27* (3): 415–32.

2020. "Performance, Satisfaction, or Loss Aversion? A Meso–Micro Assessment of Local Commitments to Sustainability Programs." *Journal of Public Administration Research and Theory 31* (1): 201–17.

Deslatte, Aaron, António Tavares, and Richard C. Feiock. 2016. "Policy of Delay: Evidence from a Bayesian Analysis of Metropolitan Land-Use Choices." *Policy Studies Journal 46* (3): 674–99.

Deslatte, Aaron, Laura Helmke-Long, John M. Anderies et al. 2021. "Assessing Sustainability through the Institutional Grammar of Urban Water Systems." *Policy Studies Journal 50* (2): 387–406.

Druckman, James N. 2001. "On the Limits of Framing Effects: Who Can Frame?" *The Journal of Politics 63* (4): 1041–66.

2004. "Political Preference Formation: Competition, Deliberation, and the (Ir)relevance of Framing Effects." *The American Political Science Review 98* (4): 671–86.

Druckman, James N., Jordan Fein, and Thomas J. Leeper. 2012. "A Source of Bias in Public Opinion Stability." *The American Political Science Review 106* (2): 430–54.

Dzigbede, Komla, Sarah Beth Gehl, and Katherine Willoughby. 2020. "Disaster Resiliency of U.S. Local Governments: Insights to Strengthen Local Response and Recovery from the COVID-19 Pandemic." *Public Administration Review 80* (4): 634–43.

Elgert, Laureen. 2018. "Rating the Sustainable City: 'Measurementality', Transparency, and Unexpected Outcomes at the Knowledge-Policy Interface." *Environmental Science & Policy 79* (January): 16–24.

Emerson, Kirk, Tina Nabatchi, and Stephen Balogh. 2012. "An Integrative Framework for Collaborative Governance." *Journal of Public Administration Research and Theory 22* (1): 1–29.

Fairfield, Tasha, and Andrew E. Charman. 2017. "Explicit Bayesian Analysis for Process Tracing: Guidelines, Opportunities, and Caveats." *Political Analysis: An Annual Publication of the Methodology Section of the American Political Science Association 25* (3): 363–80.

Feiock, Richard C., António F. Tavares, and Mark Lubell. 2008. "Policy Instrument Choices for Growth Management and Land Use Regulation." *Policy Studies Journal 36* (3): 461–80.

Fesenfeld, Lukas P., Yixian Sun, Michael Wicki, and Thomas Bernauer. 2021. "The Role and Limits of Strategic Framing for Promoting Sustainable Consumption and Policy." *Global Environmental Change: Human and Policy Dimensions 68* (May): Article 102266.

Fiorino, Daniel J. 2010. "Sustainability as a Conceptual Focus for Public Administration." *Public Administration Review 70* (s1): s78–s88.

Frederickson, H. George, and Rosemary O'Leary. 2014. "Local Government Management: Change, Crossing Boundaries, and Reinvigorating Scholarship." *American Review of Public Administration 44* (4 suppl.): 3S–10S.

Gaynor, Tia Sherèe, and Meghan E. Wilson. 2020. "Social Vulnerability and Equity: The Disproportionate Impact of COVID-19." *Public Administration Review 80* (5): 832–38.

George, Bert, Richard M. Walker, and Joost Monster. 2019. "Does Strategic Planning Improve Organizational Performance? A Meta-Analysis." *Public Administration 79* (6): 810–19.

George, Bert, Martin Baekgaard, Adelien Decramer, Mieke Audenaert, and Stijn Goeminne. 2020. "Institutional Isomorphism, Negativity Bias and Performance Information Use by Politicians: A Survey Experiment." *Public Administration 98* (1): 14–28.

Ghalayini, Alaa M., and James S. Noble. 1996. "The Changing Basis of Performance Measurement." *International Journal of Operations & Production Management 16* (8): 63–80.

Gill, Jeff. 2021. "Political Science Is a Data Science." *The Journal of Politics 83* (1): 1–7.

Godschalk, David R. 2004. "Land Use Planning Challenges: Coping with Conflicts in Visions of Sustainable Development and Livable Communities." *Journal of the American Planning Association. American Planning Association 70* (1): 5–13.

Griggs, Gary. 2021. "Rising Seas in California – an Update on Sea-Level Rise Science." In Jan W. Dash, ed., *World Scientific Encyclopedia of Climate Change*, vol. 3. World Scientific, 105–11.

Gross, Kimberly. 2008. "Framing Persuasive Appeals: Episodic and Thematic Framing, Emotional Response, and Policy Opinion." *Political Psychology 29* (2): 169–92.

Hawkins, Christopher V. 2011. "Smart Growth Policy Choice: A Resource Dependency and Local Governance Explanation." *Policy Studies Journal 39* (4): 679–707.

Hawkins, Christopher V., Rachel M. Krause, and Aaron Deslatte. 2021. "Staff Support and Administrative Capacity in Strategic Planning for Local Sustainability." *Public Management Review.* https://doi.org/10.1080/14719037.2021.1999667.

Hawkins, Christopher V., Rachel M. Krause, Richard C. Feiock, and Cali Curley. 2016. "Making Meaningful Commitments: Accounting for Variation in Cities' Investments of Staff and Fiscal Resources to Sustainability." *Urban Studies 53* (9): 1902–24.

Heyerdahl, Carl L. 1954. "Indiana Still Seeks Home Rule." *National Municipal Review 43* (4): 182–207.

Honig, Dan. 2018. "Case Study Design and Analysis as a Complementary Empirical Strategy to Econometric Analysis in the Study of Public Agencies: Deploying Mutually Supportive Mixed Methods." *Journal of Public Administration Research and Theory 29* (2): 299–317.

Howell-Moroney, Michael. 2008. "The Tiebout Hypothesis 50 Years Later: Lessons and Lingering Challenges for Metropolitan Governance in the 21st Century." *Public Administration Review 68* (1): 97–109.

Hughes, Sara. 2015. "A Meta-Analysis of Urban Climate Change Adaptation Planning in the U.S." *Urban Climate 14* (1): 17–29.

2020. "Principles, Drivers, and Policy Tools for Just Climate Change Adaptation in Legacy Cities." *Environmental Science & Policy 111* (September): 35–41.

James, Oliver, and Peter John. 2007. "Public Management at the Ballot Box: Performance Information and Electoral Support for Incumbent English Local Governments." *Journal of Public Administration Research and Theory 17* (4): 567–80.

James, O., and A. Moseley. 2014."Does Performance Information about Public Services Affect Citizens' Perceptions, Satisfaction, and Voice Behaviour? Field Experiments with Absolute and Relative Performance Information."*Public Administration 92* (2): 493–511.

Jeong, Hong-Sang, and Ralph S. Brower. 2008. "Extending the Present Understanding of Organizational Sensemaking: Three Stages and Three Contexts." *Administration & Society 40* (3): 223–52.

Ji, Hyunjung, and Nicole Darnall. 2018. "All Are Not Created Equal: Assessing Local Governments' Strategic Approaches towards Sustainability." *Public Management Review 20* (1): 154–75.

Jilke, Sebastian. 2018. "Citizen Satisfaction under Changing Political Leadership: The Role of Partisan Motivated Reasoning." *Governance 31* (3): 515–33.

Johnsen, Åge. 2018. "Impacts of Strategic Planning and Management in Municipal Government: An Analysis of Subjective Survey and Objective Production and Efficiency Measures in Norway." *Public Management Review 20* (3): 397–420.

Kahneman, Daniel, and Amos Tversky. 1986. "Rational Choice and the Framing of Decisions." *Journal of Business 59* (4): 251–78.

Krause, Rachel M. 2011. "Symbolic or Substantive Policy? Measuring the Extent of Local Commitment to Climate Protection." *Environment and Planning C: Government & Policy 29* (1): 46–62.

Krause, Rachel M., and Christopher V. Hawkins. 2021. *Implementing City Sustainability: Overcoming Administrative Silos to Achieve Functional Collective Action Cities.* Temple University Press.

Krause, Rachel M., Richard C. Feiock, and Christopher V. Hawkins. 2016. "The Administrative Organization of Sustainability within Local Government." *Journal of Public Administration Research and Theory 26* (1): 113–27.

Krause, Rachel M., Christopher V. Hawkins, and Richard C. Felock. 2021. *Implementing City Sustainability: Overcoming Administrative Silos to Achieve Functional Collective Action.* Temple University Press.

Krause, Rachel M., Christopher V. Hawkins, and Angela Y. S. Park. 2019. "The Perfect Amount of Help: An Examination of the Relationship Between Capacity and Collaboration in Urban Energy and Climate Initiatives*." Urban Affairs Review 57* (2): 583–608.

Krause, Rachel M., Hongtao Yi, and Richard C. Feiock. 2016. "Applying Policy Termination Theory to the Abandonment of Climate Protection Initiatives by U.S. Local Governments." *Policy Studies Journal: The Journal of the Policy Studies Organization 44* (2): 176–95.

Krause, Rachel M., Angela Y. S. Park, Christopher V. Hawkins, and Richard C. Feiock. 2019. "The Effect of Administrative Form and Stability on Cities' Use of Greenhouse Gas Emissions Inventories as a Basis for Mitigation." *Journal of Environmental Policy & Planning 21* (6): 826–40.

Kravchuk, Robert S., and Ronald W. Schack. 1996. "Designing Effective Performance-Measurement Systems under the Government Performance and Results Act of 1993." *Public Administration Review 56* (4): 348–58.

Kwon, Myungjung, Frances S. Berry, and Richard C. Feiock. 2009. "Understanding the Adoption and Timing of Economic Development Strategies in US Cities Using Innovation and Institutional Analysis." *Journal of Public Administration Research and Theory 19* (4): 967–88.

Kwon, Myungjung, Shui-Yan Tang, and Cheongsin Kim. 2018. "Examining Strategic Sustainability Plans and Smart-Growth Land-Use Measures in California Cities." *Journal of Environmental Planning and Management 61* (9): 1570–93.

Ladyman, James, and Karoline Wiesner. 2020. "What Is a Complex System?" In *What Is a Complex System?* Yale University Press, 9–10.

Lauterpacht, Hersch. 1955. "Codification and Development of International Law*." *The American Journal of International Law 49* (1): 16–43.

Lavertu, Stéphane. 2016. "We All Need Help: 'Big Data' and the Mismeasure of Public Administration." *Public Administration Review 76* (6): 864–72.

Lee, David, Michael McGuire, and Jong Ho Kim. 2018. "Collaboration, Strategic Plans, and Government Performance: The Case of Efforts to Reduce Homelessness." *Public Management Review 20* (3): 360–76.

Leon-Moreta, Agustin. 2018. "Functional Responsibilities of Municipal Governments." *American Review of Public Administration 48* (1): 18–32.

Leslie, Heather M., Xavier Basurto, Mateja Nenadovic, Leila Sievanen, Kyle C. Cavanaugh, Juan José Cota-Nieto, Brad E. Erisman, et al. 2015. "Operationalizing the Social-Ecological Systems Framework to Assess Sustainability." *Proceedings of the National Academy of Sciences of the United States of America 112* (19): 5979–84.

Levesque, Vanessa R., Kathleen P. Bell, and Aram J. K. Calhoun. 2017. "Planning for Sustainability in Small Municipalities: The Influence of Interest Groups, Growth Patterns, and Institutional Characteristics." *Journal of Planning Education and Research 37* (3): 322–33.

Levinthal, Daniel A., and Brian Wu. 2010. "Opportunity Costs and Non-Scale Free Capabilities: Profit Maximization, Corporate Scope, and Profit Margins." *Strategic Management Journal 31* (7): 780–801.

Liao, Lu, Mildred E. Warner, and George C. Homsy. 2020. "When Do Plans Matter?" *Journal of the American Planning Association 86* (1): 60–74.

Llewellyn, Sue, and Markus J. Milne. 2007. "Accounting as Codified Discourse." *Accounting, Auditing & Accountability Journal 20* (6): 805–24.

Lowery, David. 1999. "Sorting in the Fragmented Metropolis: Updating the Social Stratification-Government Inequality Debate." *Public Management an International Journal of Research and Theory 1* (1): 7–26.

Lubell, Mark, Richard C. Feiock, and Edgar E. Ramirez de la Cruz. 2005. "Political Institutions and Conservation by Local Governments." *Urban Affairs Review 40* (6): 706–29.

Lubell, Mark, Richard C. Feiock, and Edgar E. Ramirez de la Cruz. 2009. "Local Institutions and the Politics of Urban Growth." *American Journal of Political Science 53* (3): 649–65.

Lynch, Thomas D., and Susan E. Day. 1996. "Public Sector Performance Measurement." *Public Administration Quarterly 19* (4): 404–19.

Ma, Yanni, Graham Dixon, and Jay D. Hmielowski. 2019. "Psychological Reactance From Reading Basic Facts on Climate Change: The Role of Prior Views and Political Identification." *Environmental Communication 13* (1): 71–86.

MacQueen, Kathleen M., Eleanor McLellan, Kelly Kay, and Bobby Milstein. 1998. "Codebook Development for Team-Based Qualitative Analysis." *CAMSI Journal: Journal ACEMI 10* (2): 31–36.

March, James G. 2010. *The Ambiguities of Experience.* Cornell University Press.

Mayntz, Renate. 2004. "Mechanisms in the Analysis of Social Macro-Phenomena." *Philosophy of the Social Sciences 34* (2): 237–59.

Mazmanian, Daniel A., and Michael E. Kraft. 2009. *Toward Sustainable Communities: Transition and Transformations in Environmental Policy.* MIT Press.

McGinnis, Michael D. 2011. "An Introduction to IAD and the Language of the Ostrom Workshop: A Simple Guide to a Complex Framework." *Policy Studies Journal 39* (1): 169–83.

McGinnis, Michael D., and Elinor Ostrom. 2012. "Reflections on Vincent Ostrom, Public Administration, and Polycentricity." *Public Administration Review 72* (1): 15–25.

Meier, Kenneth J., Søren C. Winter, Laurence J. O'toole Jr, Nathan Favero, and Simon Calmar Andersen. 2015. "The Validity of Subjective Performance Measures: School Principals in Texas and Denmark." *Public Administration 93* (4): 1084–101.

Miles, Matthew B., and A. Michael Huberman. 1994. *Qualitative Data Analysis: An Expanded Sourcebook*, 2nd ed. Sage Publications.

Miner, John B. 2015. *Organizational Behavior 2: Essential Theories of Process and Structure*. Routledge.

Moore, Mark Harrison. 1995. *Creating Public Value: Strategic Management in Government*. Harvard University Press.

Moynihan, Donald P. 2008. *The Dynamics of Performance Management: Constructing Information and Reform*. Georgetown University Press.

2018. "A Great Schism Approaching? Towards a Micro and Macro Public Administration." https://doi.org/10.2139/ssrn.3481460.

Moynihan, Donald P., and Stéphane Lavertu. 2012. "Does Involvement in Performance Management Routines Encourage Performance Information Use? Evaluating GPRA and PART." *Public Administration Review 72* (4): 592–602.

Moynihan, Donald P., and Sanjay K. Pandey. 2010. "The Big Question for Performance Management: Why Do Managers Use Performance Information?" *Journal of Public Administration Research and Theory 20* (4): 849–66.

Mukherjee, Sourav, Ashok Kumar Mishra, Michael E. Mann, and Colin Raymond. 2021. "Anthropogenic Warming and Population Growth May Double US Heat Stress by the Late 21st Century." *Earth's Future 9* (5). https://doi.org/10.1029/2020ef001886.

Muneepeerakul, Rachata, and John M. Anderies. 2017. "Strategic Behaviors and Governance Challenges in Social-Ecological Systems." *Earth's Future 5* (8): 865–76.

Nicholson-Crotty, Sean, Jill Nicholson-Crotty, and Sean Webeck. 2019. "Are Public Managers More Risk Averse? Framing Effects and Status Quo Bias across the Sectors." *Journal of Behavioral Public Administration 2* (1). https://doi.org/10.30636/jbpa.21.35.

Nielsen, Poul A., and Donald P. Moynihan. 2017. "How Do Politicians Attribute Bureaucratic Responsibility for Performance? Negativity Bias and Interest Group Advocacy." *Journal of Public Administration Research and Theory 27* (2): 269–83.

Niemann, Ludger, and Thomas Hoppe. 2018. "Sustainability Reporting by Local Governments: A Magic Tool? Lessons on Use and Usefulness from European Pioneers." *Public Management Review 20* (1): 201–23.

Olsen, Asmus Leth. 2015. "Citizen (Dis)satisfaction: An Experimental Equivalence Framing Study." *Public Administration Review 75* (3): 469–78.

Opp, Susan M., Samantha L. Mosier, and Jeffery L. Osgood Jr. 2018. *Performance Measurement in Local Sustainability Policy*. Routledge.

Ostrom, Elinor. 1983. "The Social Stratification-Government Inequality Thesis Explored." *Urban Affairs Quarterly 19* (1): 91–112.

1990. *Governing the Commons: The Evolution of Institutions for Collective Action.* Cambridge University Press.

2010. "Polycentric Systems for Coping with Collective Action and Global Environmental Change." *Global Environmental Change: Human and Policy Dimensions 20* (4): 550–57.

2011. "Background on the Institutional Analysis and Development Framework." *Policy Studies Journal: The Journal of the Policy Studies Organization 39* (1): 7–27.

Ostrom, Vincent, and Barbara Allen. 2008. *The Political Theory of a Compound Republic: Designing the American Experiment.* Lexington Books.

Ostrom, Vincent, and Elinor Ostrom. 1965. "A Behavioral Approach to the Study of Intergovernmental Relations." *The Annals of the American Academy of Political and Social Science 359* (1): 137–46.

2019. "Public Goods and Public Choices." In E. S. Savas, ed., *Alternatives for Delivering Public Services.* Routledge, 7–49.

O'Toole Jr., Laurence J. and Meier, Kenneth J., 1999. "Modeling the Impact of Public Management: Implications of Structural Context." *Journal of Public Administration Research and Theory 9* (4):505–26.

Oxley, Z. 2020. "Framing and Political Decision Making: An Overview." *Oxford Research Encyclopedia of Politics.* https://oxfordre.com/view/10.1093/acrefore/9780190228637.001.0001/acrefore-9780190228637-e-1250.

Park, Angela Y. S., and Rachel M. Krause. 2020. "Exploring the Landscape of Sustainability Performance Management Systems in U.S. Local Governments." *Journal of Environmental Management* 279: 111764. https://doi.org/10.1016/j.jenvman.2020.111764.

Park, Angela Y. S., Rachel M. Krause, and Christopher V. Hawkins. 2020. "Institutional Mechanisms for Local Sustainability Collaboration: Assessing the Duality of Formal and Informal Mechanisms in Promoting Collaborative Processes." *Journal of Public Administration Research and Theory 31* (2): 434–50. https://doi.org/10.1093/jopart/muaa036.

Pennington, Mark. 2000. *Planning and the Political Market: Public Choice and the Politics of Government Failure.* A&C Black.

Piening, Erk P. 2013. "Dynamic Capabilities in Public Organizations: A Literature Review and Research Agenda." *Public Management Review 15* (2): 209–45.

Poister, Theodore H. 2010. "The Future of Strategic Planning in the Public Sector: Linking Strategic Management and Performance." *Public Administration Review 70* (s1): s246–54.

Poister, Theodore H., and Gregory Streib. 1999. "Performance Measurement in Municipal Government: Assessing the State of the Practice." *Public Administration Review 59* (4): 325–35.

Portney, Kent. 2005. "Civic Engagement and Sustainable Cities in the United States." *Public Administration Review 65* (5): 579–91.

Portney, Kent E. 2013. *Taking Sustainable Cities Seriously: Economic Development, the Environment, and Quality of Life in American Cities*. MIT Press.

Radin, Beryl. 2006. *Challenging the Performance Movement: Accountability, Complexity, and Democratic Values*. Georgetown University Press.

Rivas, Susan Barnhizer. 1983. "The Indiana Home Rule Act: A Second Chance for Local Self-Government." *Indiana Law Review 16* (3): 677–704.

Rosenberg Hansen, Jesper, and Ewan Ferlie. 2016. "Applying Strategic Management Theories in Public Sector Organizations: Developing a Typology." *Public Management Review 18* (1): 1–19.

Rubin, Herbert J. 1986. "Local Economic Development Organizations and the Activities of Small Cities in Encouraging Economic Growth." *Policy Studies Journal 14* (3): 363–88.

Siciliano, Michael D., Nienke M. Moolenaar, Alan J. Daly, and Yi-Hwa Liou. 2017. "A Cognitive Perspective on Policy Implementation: Reform Beliefs, Sensemaking, and Social Networks." *Public Administration Review 77* (6): 889–901.

Simon, Herbert A. 1988. "The Science of Design: Creating the Artificial." *Design Issues 4* (1/2): 67–82.

1996. *The Sciences of the Artificial*. MIT Press.

1997. *Models of Bounded Rationality: Empirically Grounded Economic Reason*. MIT Press.

Slothuus, Rune. 2008. "More than Weighting Cognitive Importance: A Dual-Process Model of Issue Framing Effects." *Political Psychology 29* (1): 1–28.

Slothuus, Rune, and Claes H. de Vreese. 2010. "Political Parties, Motivated Reasoning, and Issue Framing Effects." *The Journal of Politics 72* (3): 630–45.

Stazyk, Edmund C., Alisa Moldavanova, and H. George Frederickson. 2016. "Sustainability, Intergenerational Social Equity, and the Socially Responsible Organization." *Administration & Society 48* (6): 655–82.

Stokan, Eric, and Aaron Deslatte. 2020. "Beyond Borders: Governmental Fragmentation and the Political Market for Growth in American Cities." *State and Local Government Review 51* (3): 150–67.

Swann, William L. 2017. "Examining the Impact of Local Collaborative Tools on Urban Sustainability Efforts: Does the Managerial Environment Matter?" *American Review of Public Administration 47* (4): 455–68.

Tajudeen, Yusuf, and Iyiola Oladunjoye. 2021. "Climate Change—An Emblematic Driver of Vector-Borne Diseases: Holistic View As A Way Forward." *Global Biosecurity 3* (1). http://doi.org/10.31646/gbio .120.

Teske, Paul, Mark Schneider, Michael Mintrom, and Samuel Best. 1993. "Establishing The Micro Foundations of a Macro Theory: Information, Movers, and the Competitive Local Market for Public Goods." *The American Political Science Review 87* (3): 702–13.

Tilbury, Clare. 2004. "The Influence of Performance Measurement on Child Welfare Policy and Practice." *British Journal of Social Work 34* (2): 225–41.

Tubridy, Daniel, Mark Scott, and Mick Lennon. 2021. "Managed Retreat in Response to Flooding: Lessons from the Past for Contemporary Climate Change Adaptation." *Planning Perspectives 36* (6): 1249–68.

Tuchman, Gaye. 1978. *Making News: A Study in the Construction of Reality.* Free Press.

Van Dooren, Wouter, and Steven Van de Walle. 2016. *Performance Information in the Public Sector: How It Is Used.* Springer.

Vlaev, Ivo, Dominic King, Paul Dolan, and Ara Darzi. 2016. "The Theory and Practice of 'Nudging': Changing Health Behaviors." *Public Administration Review 76* (4): 550–61.

Wagner, Claudia, Markus Strohmaier, Alexandra Olteanu et al. 2021. "Measuring Algorithmically Infused Societies." *Nature 595* (7866): 197–204.

Walker, Richard M. 2014. "Internal and External Antecedents of Process Innovation: A Review and Extension." *Public Management Review 16* (1): 21–44.

Wang, Xiaohu. 2002. "Assessing Performance Measurement Impact: A Study of US Local Governments." *Public Performance & Management Review 26* (1): 26–43.

Wang, Xiaohu, Christopher V. Hawkins, Nick Lebredo, and Evan M. Berman. 2012. "Capacity to Sustain Sustainability: A Study of US Cities." *Public Administration Review 72* (6): 841–53.

Watson, Siobhan. 2020. "Building on Local Successes: The Energy Efficiency and Conservation Block Grant Program and Its Lessons for Federal Climate Policy." Doctoral thesis, Columbia University. https://academic commons.columbia.edu/doi/10.7916/d8-f5kb-9b94.

Weick, Karl E. 1995. *Sensemaking in Organizations*. SAGE.

——— 2015. Review of *The Social Psychology of Organizing*, by Karl E. Weick. *M@N@Gement 18* (2): 189–93.

Weick, Karl E., Kathleen M. Sutcliffe, and David Obstfeld. 2005. "Organizing and the Process of Sensemaking." *Organization Science 16* (4): 409–21.

Winter, Sidney G., and Gabriel Szulanski. 2001. "Replication as Strategy." *Organization Science 12* (6): 730–43.

Winter, Sidney G., and Gabriel Szulanski. 2002. Getting It Right the Second Time. *Harvard Business Review*. January. https://hbr.org/2002/01/getting-it-right-the-second-time.

Yi, Hongtao, Rachel M. Krause, and Richard C. Feiock. 2017. "Back-Pedaling or Continuing Quietly? Assessing the Impact of ICLEI Membership Termination on Cities' Sustainability Actions." *Environmental Politics 26* (1): 138–60. https://doi.org/10.1080/09644016.2016.1244968.

Yi, Hongtao, Liming Suo, Ruowen Shen, Jiasheng Zhang, Anu Ramaswami, and Richard C. Feiock. 2018. "Regional Governance and Institutional Collective Action for Environmental Sustainability." *Public Administration Review 78* (4): 556–66.

Zander, Udo, and Bruce Kogut. 1995. "Knowledge and the Speed of the Transfer and Imitation of Organizational Capabilities: An Empirical Test." *Organization Science 6* (1): 76–92.

Zeemering, Eric S. 2018. "Sustainability Management, Strategy and Reform in Local Government." *Public Management Review 20* (1): 136–53.

Zhang, Jiasheng, Hui Li, and Kaifeng Yang. 2022. "Explaining Sustainability Innovation in City Governments: Innovation Mechanisms and Discretion Types in Multi-Level Governance." *American Review of Public Administration 52* (5): 366–81.

Zollo, Maurizio, and Sidney G. Winter. 2002. "Deliberate Learning and the Evolution of Dynamic Capabilities." *Organization Science 13* (3): 339–51.

Acknowledgments

This research was supported by the National Science Foundation (Award # **1941561**).

About the Author

Aaron Deslatte is an assistant professor at Indiana University Bloomington, where he directs the Metropolitan Governance and Management Transitions (MGMT) Lab. He is also a faculty affiliate with the Vincent and Elinor Ostrom Workshop. His research focuses on the organizational and institutional challenges associated with local sustainability, resilience, and climate-action in metropolitan regions. This transdisciplinary work explores questions of governance and management from a systems perspective to help make sense of the linkages between the environment and human institutions and behavior.

Cambridge Elements ⹀

Public and Nonprofit Administration

Andrew Whitford
University of Georgia

Andrew Whitford is Alexander M. Crenshaw Professor of Public Policy in the School of Public and International Affairs at the University of Georgia. His research centers on strategy and innovation in public policy and organization studies.

Robert Christensen
Brigham Young University

Robert Christensen is Professor and George Romney Research Fellow in the Marriott School at Brigham Young University. His research focuses on prosocial and antisocial behaviors and attitudes in public and nonprofit organizations.

About the Series

The foundation of this series are cutting-edge contributions on emerging topics and definitive reviews of keystone topics in public and nonprofit administration, especially those that lack longer treatment in textbook or other formats. Among keystone topics of interest for scholars and practitioners of public and nonprofit administration, it covers public management, public budgeting and finance, nonprofit studies, and the interstitial space between the public and nonprofit sectors, along with theoretical and methodological contributions, including quantitative, qualitative, and mixed-methods pieces.

The Public Management Research Association

The Public Management Research Association improves public governance by advancing research on public organizations, strengthening links among interdisciplinary scholars, and furthering professional and academic opportunities in public management.

Cambridge Elements $^{\equiv}$

Public and Nonprofit Administration

.

Printed in the United States
by Baker & Taylor Publisher Services